FRANZ KAFKA

LITERATURE AND LIFE:
WORLD WRITERS

Selected list of titles in this series:

ALFRED ADLER	*Josef Rattner*
S. Y. AGNON	*Harold Fisch*
JEAN ANOUILH	*Louis J. Falb*
ISAAC BABEL	*Richard Hallett*
SIMONE DE BEAUVOIR	*Robert D. Cottrell*
JORGE LUIS BORGES	*George R. McMurray*
BERT BRECHT	*Willy Haas*
ANTON CHEKHOV	*Siegfried Melchinger*
PAUL CLAUDEL	*Bettina L. Knapp*
COLETTE	*Robert D. Cottrell*
JULIO CORTÁZAR	*Evelyn Picon Garfield*
EURIPIDES	*Siegfried Melchinger*
CARLOS FUENTES	*Wendy B. Faris*
FEDERICO GARCÍA LORCA	*Felicia Hardison Londré*
GABRIEL GARCÍA MÁRQUEZ	*George R. McMurray*
GÜNTER GRASS	*Richard H. Lawson*
ANDRÉ MALRAUX	*James Robert Hewitt*
MOLIÈRE	*Gertrud Mander*
RAINER MARIA RILKE	*Arnold Bauer*
FRIEDRICH SCHILLER	*Charles E. Passage*
MARIO VARGAS LLOSA	*Raymond Leslie Williams*
SIMONE WEIL	*Dorothy Tuck McFarland*

Complete list of titles in the series available from the publisher on request.

FRANZ KAFKA

Richard H. Lawson

UNGAR · NEW YORK

1987

The Ungar Publishing Company
370 Lexington Avenue, New York, NY 10017

Printed in the United States of America

Library of Congress Cataloging-in-Publication Data

Lawson, Richard H.
  Franz Kafka.

  (Literature and life series)
  Bibliography: p.
  Includes index.
  1. Kafka, Franz, 1883–1924—Criticism and interpreta-
tion. I. Title. II. Series.
Pt2621.A26Z7674 1987   833'.912   87–5873
ISBN 0–8044–2502–7

Contents

Chronology   vii
Introduction   1
1 Early Prose: *Description of a Struggle,*
  "Wedding Preparations in the Country,"
  "The Judgment"   15
2 *The Metamorphosis,* "The Stoker"   27
3 *Amerika*   39
4 *The Trial*   55
5 "In the Penal Colony," "A Country Doctor,"
  "An Old Manuscript," "Building the
  Great Wall of China," "A Report for
  an Academy"   87
6 *The Castle*   103
7 "Investigations of a Dog," "The Burrow,"
  "A Hunger Artist," "Josephine
  the Singer"   125
8 The Parables   139
Conclusions   151
Notes   157
Bibliography   161
Index   167

Chronology

1883	Born on July 3 in Prague.
1888–93	Attends German elementary school.
1896	Celebrates bar mitzvah.
1893–1901	Attends German preparatory school.
1901–6	Studies law at German university in Prague.
1902	Begins to write prose sketches; meets Max Brod.
1906	Completes law degree; begins insurance work at Assicurazioni Generali.
1908	Begins work at Workers' Accident Insurance Institute.
1910	Develops interest in Yiddish theater; starts diary; writes first drafts of *Amerika*.
1912	Meets Felice Bauer; writes "The Judgment" and *The Metamorphosis*; completes first seven chapters of *Amerika*.
1914	Becomes engaged to Felice (engagement broken the same year); moves from parents' home; writes *The Trial* (incomplete) and "In the Penal Colony"; meets Grete Bloch.
1915	Kafka's son supposedly born to Grete Bloch—unknown to Kafka.

1917   Again becomes engaged to Felice (engagement bro-
            ken after five months); diagnosed as having tubercu-
            losis; moves to the country with sister Ottla; writes
            numerous stories and parables, including "A Country
            Doctor," "Building the Great Wall of China," "A Re-
            port for an Academy," and "The New Attorney."

1918   Returns to Prague and goes on half-time at insurance
            institute; meets Julie Wohryzek.

1919   Becomes engaged to Julie; writes "Letter to His Fa-
            ther" (unsent).

1920   Falls in love with Milena Jesenská and breaks with
            Julie; writes first sketch for *The Castle*.

1922   As tuberculosis worsens, tells Max Brod to destroy
            his work after he dies; retires on pension from insur-
            ance institute; writes much of *The Castle* as well as
            stories and parables, including "Investigations of a
            Dog," "A Hunger Artist," and "On Parables."

1923   Lives in Berlin with Dora Dymant; writes "The Bur-
            row" and "Josephine the Singer."

1924   Dies on June 3 at Kierling Sanatorium near Kloster-
            neuburg, Austria.

FRANZ KAFKA

Introduction

Franz Kafka's life began in Prague, in the house "By the Tower" on the corner of Maisl and Kapr Streets, on the very edge of the former ghetto, on July 3, 1883. It was to end a short forty-one years later, on June 3, 1924, at Kierling Sanatorium near Klosterneuburg, Austria. At the time of Kafka's birth, Prague was a large provincial capital in the Austro-Hungarian empire, a realm of many nationalities and many races, including, in Prague, Czechs, Germans, and German Jews — the latter two groups combined making up no more than 10 percent of the city's populace.

Though not so early as in Germany, the gradual emancipation of the Jews in the empire ruled by the Austrian Hapsburgs was materially completed by the formal abolition of the ghettos in 1852, just one generation before Franz Kafka — in fact 1852 was the birth date of his father Hermann Kafka. Hermann sometimes spelled his given name as Herman with a single *n* in the Czech fashion. And the surname, hardly more than two or three generations old in 1852, is undoubtedly Czech: *kavka* is the Czech word for "jackdaw." In spite of his Czech name, Hermann Kafka was among the typically ardent Germanizers in the minority Jewish community in Prague. Fluent in his mother tongue, Czech, his Yiddish atrophied to a nucleus of expletives, he insisted — there was never any doubt — on a thorough German education for Franz, his only son to survive infancy. In that direction lay the prospect of further social and professional advancement, accompanied by an even greater degree of bourgeois security.

1

Because Hermann Kafka looms larger than life in the writings of his son, there is some advantage in examining the circumstances of the father before we proceed to the life of his son. One of six children, Hermann Kafka endured poverty and physical hardship in the south Bohemian village of Osek—in German Wossek or Wohsek—before he was sent off on his own at the age of fourteen. He had learned German at the village Jewish school—which seems to have been a Jewish educational center for a considerable region. By the time he left home, however, he had already given up the religious observances of Judaism. He served a three-year hitch in the Imperial and Royal Army beginning when he was nineteen. The language of command in this multiethnic military force was German, and Hermann Kafka became a platoon leader.

When his hitch was completed, he took up the career of an itinerant trader, ultimately settling in Prague. In this move to the provincial capital he typified the nineteenth-century migration of the Central European Jews (of course not only of the Jews) from countryside to city. His marriage too was typical: the poor but ambitious émigré from the country married Julie Löwy, daughter of a prosperous and stable family of merchants, members of the German-Jewish establishment. Aided by Löwy's funds and his own driving ambition and willingness to work hard for material security, Hermann Kafka set up a haberdashery business. His success matched his ambition. While he may never have felt deep within that his bourgeois status was safe, it was.

There were three sons. Franz's two younger brothers, born in 1885 and 1887, died in infancy. Three younger sisters were born in 1889, 1890, and 1892. (They were to be murdered in the Holocaust.) From very early there seems to have been an absence of sympathy—to put it mildly—between the father, all too harsh and all too concerned about his business, and Franz, all too sensitive to the absent pater-

nal love (or perhaps only badly misdirected). This estrangement Julie Kafka was unable to mediate in any very helpful
way. Franz, feeling himself badgered, threatened, and si-
lenced, followed his probably natural bent to turn inward.

Added to the unsettledness of his personal existence
were the frequent moves of the Kafka family as it grew and
its means became considerable. Not that the moves were to
distant neighborhoods. With the exception of a few months
in Wenceslas Square in 1885 they were all in the vicinity of
Old Town Square, itself not far removed from the former
ghetto. The latter — partly deteriorated, partly rebuilt — was a
poverty-stricken area, in the last years of the nineteenth century still referred to as V *židech* (Among the Jews) or *Za
drátem* (Behind the Wire).[1] As a schoolboy, Kafka was familiar with its byways, from which all but the very poorest Jews
had moved half a century earlier.

At the age of six, Franz began attending the German —
as opposed to the neighboring Czech — school. It was the
family's cook who walked him to school. His father was busy;
his mother was busy, not only giving birth to younger sisters
but also working in the family business. The cook threatened to denounce Franz to the teacher as an unruly boy at
home; even if she didn't follow through, the boy was keenly
aware of her power to do so. A precarious existence. If the
cook was late in fetching him after school he would get
involved in youthful brawls on the street — thus of course
certifying his purported unruliness.

The cook, one of an ever-changing cast of family servants who entered and left the boy's life, was Czech — and
until Franz began school he spoke more Czech than German. The only stability in this quarter was afforded by the
long tenure of Marie Werner as governess; she was Jewish —
and spoke Czech, not German.

At the age of ten, the youngster Kafka entered the Alt-
städter Deutsches Gymnasium, whose name tells us that

the school was in Old Town, in the neighborhood of the Kafka family's places of residence and that it was German. Franz early had the reputation of being a loner. Three-fourths of his classmates were Jewish, to whose academic feats he reacted with a mixture of indifference, fear, and guilt. Not that he was a poor student himself; in fact, despite his subsequent adult disparagement of his efforts, he was an excellent student. And not that he was completely unsociable either; he just held back from taking any social initiatives. The curriculum was rigorous but unbalanced: Czech, Latin, history, Greek, Hebrew, religion, and natural history (but hardly any mathematics) were taught; and attrition among the pupils was steady.

Hermann Kafka's Judaism may have been tepid, but he had his only son Franz celebrate his bar mitzvah. Though Franz memorized what had to be memorized, the ceremony meant nothing to him as far as his faith was concerned, for he was already avowedly atheistic. What did begin to mean something to him was his interest in the German theater in Prague. Naturalistic drama was in the ascendant at this point. Kafka's interest was not merely that of a passive spectator, or even a schoolboy critic, but included the writing of scenarios to be acted out by his sisters at home. He also wrote fragments of a novel. Probably theater and writing, as well as general academic excellence provided him with a kind of counterweight against what he felt to be paternal persecution. In any event writing itself was to become one of the many bones of contention between father and son, indeed practically a symbol of all the other disharmonies by which they were alienated.

In 1901 Kafka began his studies at the German university in Prague. The Charles-Ferdinand University, founded in 1348, was in Kafka's day — in fact beginning just two years before his birth — divided into two parts, German and Czech. Enrollment in the German university was the route to professional and social success for the sons of the German-speaking Jews of Prague.

Having earlier announced the intention of studying philosophy, the matriculant enrolled in chemistry for two weeks; after one semester of Germanic studies he switched to law. The uncertainty about his field of study suggests an indifference that was probably genuine. But at least law was a field of which his father approved and which offered no small range of future employment prospects. And the boring law lectures did not prevent him from also attending lectures on art history, literature, and philosophy. Nor from making new friends, among them Max Brod, his lifelong friend and later literary executor. Nor from his initial somewhat furtive and guilt-ridden sexual relationship with a young woman — and subsequently, and more satisfyingly, with an older woman.

Coping with multifarious demands on his time and energy, of which those relating to legal study were certainly antipathetic, Kafka in 1905 made his first acquaintance with a sanatorium, in Zuckmantel in Moravian Silesia. (So far his only foreign travel had consisted of a trip to the German North Sea islands of Norderney and Helgoland shortly after his graduation from *Gymnasium*.) On returning to Prague, he resumed his studies and passed his second battery of examinations. Thus qualified for a period of compulsory unpaid paralegal work, he was taken on by a lawyer with offices in the familiar precincts of Old Town. Within three months Kafka passed his final examinations; on June 18, 1907, he received his doctorate in law.

Only a short time thereafter, following an unprecedented eleven years at one residence, the Kafka family moved once more. One would have thought that this might be the moment when the soon-to-be twenty-four-year-old lawyer-son would look for quarters of his own, even if it were in anticipation of a job that he did not yet have. But no, he chose to remain in the troublesome role of adult son in a crowded flat under the parental roof—and under the parental eye as well. After the family move and a vacation with his uncle in Triesch (including summer romances with two girls) he went to work on October 1 for the Assicurazioni Generali, an insurance office in Prague.

It was not a post conducive to the leisure necessary for his writing. Office hours, six days a week, were from 8 to 6:15 (with a two-hour midday break), the work was dull, the environment abrasive, and he found little in common with his coworkers. His only hope lay in a transfer to Trieste—in anticipation of which he was studying Italian. When hopes for the transfer dimmed, he began looking for a better job, one not only more tolerable in itself but one that would allow him sufficient time and energy to write. In March 1908 he had published his first short prose pieces, but the prospect for following up on this debut was not auspicious for an employee of Assicurazioni Generali.

In July he took a new and better post in Prague with the Workers' Accident Insurance Institute for the Kingdom of Bohemia, a semigovernmental agency. He had prepared himself for this kind of insurance work by taking a course on workmen's compensation. The salary here was superior, his workday ended at 2, he advanced rapidly, both professionally and in the esteem of his colleagues. His work had to do with the settlement of workers' compensation claims, it involved using Czech as well as German, and it involved at least occasional short trips away from Prague. (Referring to the tenacious influence of his native city, he was later to declare: "This little mother has claws.") His reports reveal that his work gave more than a little play to his essential humanitarianism as well as to his bent for close observation.

His new job also gave him the opportunity to deepen his friendship with Max Brod and to do literary writing. It was Brod, so unlike Kafka in personality and literary style (sentimental and facile, versus Kafka, spare and perfectionistic)—it was Brod who urged Kafka to write and to publish. But what Kafka's new job conferred in the way of time and energy for writing, was almost immediately taken away by the demands of family—above all his father—and the family business. Health problems of father, mother, and grandfather, the shouting and the harassment by his father, the din, the family traffic through his room, his own exhaustion in the face of all this—made writing a difficult feat.

What Kafka had written while he was a law student was principally a series of short prose pieces, most of which—with Brod urging Kafka at every step—found publication in periodicals in 1908 and 1909, when Kafka was beginning his employment at the Workers' Accident Insurance Institute. There was also from early 1907 a novel, *Description of a Struggle*, in two versions, neither of which was brought to completion, nor was another short work probably intended to be a novel, "Wedding Preparations in the Country," which exists in three unfinished versions.

Now, after approximately two years in his new post, still struggling against the circumstances at home—from which, however, he did not move—he was writing more short pieces, had begun keeping a diary, and was busy with the first draft of another novel, *Lost without Trace*, which Max Brod published still incomplete after Kafka's death under the title *Amerika*.

Coincident with the beginning of his diary was Kafka's discovery of and interest in the Polish Yiddish Musical Drama Company, which was to have a run of several months in Prague. If Kafka's infrequent involvement with the religion of Judaism only reinforced his long-held negative feelings about Jewishness—both his own and that of others—this austere Yiddish theater was a source of enlightenment and excitement about the interrelationship of the various aspects of Jewish culture.

It was on August 13, 1912, that Kafka first met his future fiancée, Felice Bauer, at the home of Max Brod, to whose family she was distantly related. She was visiting from Berlin. How she first appeared to him Kafka was able to describe with his usual — in fact, unflattering — objectivity. But before the evening was over he was attracted to her to the point of awkwardness — or rather he was more than usually conscious of what he imagined was his customary maladroitness. Almost two years later he and Felice Bauer became engaged.

Shortly after meeting Felice, he wrote "The Judgment," which introduced a period of stop-and-go creative maturity that ended only with his death twelve years later. In the same year he completed *The Metamorphosis*, the first seven chapters of a revised version of *Lost without Trace*, including "The Stoker," which was published separately as a novella in 1913.

It was about this time that he first read Kierkegaard's "Fear and Trembling."[2] Then his creative work seems to have yielded to an intense on-again, off-again correspondence with Felice Bauer that bespoke his intense self-doubt in that quarter. The correspondence was punctuated by an uncharacteristic decisiveness when Kafka early in 1914 went to Berlin to see her. His two-day visit resulted in even greater doubt and mutual misunderstanding. Yet only four months later their engagement was officially announced. And was broken, by Kafka, three months after that. From his letters and diaries it seems clear that the reason for his doubts lay in his perception of the incompatibility between his writing and the demands of middle-class domesticity. One may further glean from the testimony of his letters that he regarded writing as the means by which he could escape the intolerabilities of a life that he likened to an underworld.

Nonetheless, at about the same time that he was expressing his plight in such dire terms, halfway into 1914,

Kafka and Felice Bauer became once more unofficially engaged. The effect on him of World War I, which erupted in the summer of 1914, was somewhat remote – and continued to remain so. He was exempted from the general mobilization of Austria-Hungary by virtue of his "essential civilian function" with the semigovernmental insurance company. After a depressing trip to Hungary in 1915 and an equally depressing return to Prague, he attempted to enlist in the army but was rejected.

By now he had completed writing the novella "In the Penal Colony" and had started working on the novel *The Trial*. At long last, in August 1914, at the age of thirty-one, Kafka moved from his parents' home. His new quarters (changed again in a month) provided no surcease from noise and disturbance, but he was quite able to contrast – and compare – his private suffering with the larger, war-imposed suffering of his brother-in-law and of the community in general. His uncertain relationship with Felice Bauer continued, mediated by Felice's girlfriend Grete Bloch – who later asserted that Kafka was the father of her son.

By 1916 his agreement with Felice was that they would marry when the war was over and live in Berlin. Under the stringency of war his employer lengthened his hours of work. At the same time, in the absence of his brothers-in-law, the family-owned asbestos factory (opened in 1911) demanded – or in its name his father demanded – more of his energy and attention. Small wonder that Kafka, desperately nervous from insomnia and headaches, overcame his aversion to doctors sufficiently to seek a consultation – or that 1916 was not a year in which he did much writing.

It was different the following year. Among his amazing outpouring of short fiction are: "A Country Doctor," "Jackals and Arabs," "The Hunter Gracchus," "Building the Great Wall of China," "A Message from the Emperor" (an extract from the preceding), "A Report for an Academy," and "The

Neighbor." At the same period he was beginning to block out the novel *The Castle*.

Shortly after the second engagement between Kafka and Felice Bauer was made official, Kafka's incipient tuberculosis was diagnosed as bronchitis. The patient himself knew better, however. He tended to cast his affliction in psychosomatic terms as the definitive triumph of evil in his five-year battle for Felice. As before, though this time more finally, after a few months the engagement was broken. By then Kafka, on the basis of a medical certification, was on an extended paid leave of absence from his insurance work. During this eight-month recuperative—at any rate happy—period he lived with his youngest sister Ottla on their brother-in-law's farm in Zürau, a village in northwestern Bohemia.

He returned to Prague only to fall victim, a few months later, to the influenza epidemic then raging worldwide. He was in bed for three weeks; shortly thereafter he obtained a further medical leave to convalesce in the countryside, at Schelesen (Zelizy). In October 1918 Czechoslovakia was declared a republic, and in November the Hapsburg monarchy, the political and racial framework in which Kafka had been born and lived, came to its end.

On a second stay in Schelesen Kafka met Julie Wohryzek, daughter of a Jewish shoemaker and synagogue official in Prague. Possessor of a keen wit himself, Kafka seems to have met his match in the good-natured Julie. Within a few months they became engaged, much to the outrage of Kafka's father at the alliance with a socially inferior family. The wedding, scheduled for November, did not take place, however. Kafka's fear of marriage and its effect on his writing probably stood in no need of paternal reinforcement (even if on a very different basis). This is the immediate background of Kafka's well-known "Letter to His Father."

Never sent—or more likely never handed on to his father by his mother—this letter of over a hundred pages is as

rich in self-accusation as in accusation of the "dearest father" to whom it was addressed. Kafka accuses himself of
being oversensitively fearful in the face of his father's unreflective, instinctive self-aggrandizement. It is not a fair, chiv-
alrous fight between them, not a fight between honorable
opponents, but one in which the letter writer is confronted
by a bloodsucking vermin. He draws two distinct character
types: the son, more a Löwy than a Kafka, odd, shy, quiet;
the father, a Kafka through and through, forceful, strong,
noisy, knowledgeable, unreflective — all those attributes that
are necessary, as the son sees it, for a tolerable bourgeois
marriage — and that he so significantly lacks.

Kafka asserts that he was essentially raised by his domi-
neering father, as a result of which he, the son, lost his
natural self-confidence, which was replaced by a sense of
guilt. Whatever Franz did or wanted to do was opposed or
ridiculed by Hermann. Even when Franz became interested
in his Jewish roots and in Judaism, that too attracted the
father's hostility; although the father ought to have wel-
comed a fruitful topic for discussion, his own Judaism consisting only of formalized, meaningless fragments.

Of course it is easy to put a Freudian light on this
picture, but Franz Kafka, who knew his early Freud, did not.
From the critical reader's point of view it probably suffices to
keep this tormented father-son relationship in mind while
considering Kafka's fiction — but also to bear in mind that
the relationship is as perceived by the son, that Kafka senior,
while doubtless a domestic tyrant and certainly a self-made
man, was not after all a complete monster in the eyes of
witnesses other than his aggrieved son. It is not entirely
dialectic to suggest that there was an element of love, of
admiration as well as disdain in their relationship, which, as
far as personal contact went, deteriorated into a virtual non-
relationship after Kafka finally left the paternal roof.

Despite the unpromising prospects explicit and implicit

in the letter, Kafka's engagement with Julie Wohryzek was not immediately broken. She had the further misfortune of still going with Kafka not only during the period of his somewhat paternal relationship with Minze Eisner but also during the early period of his love for Milena Jesenská Poláková.

He began writing — Kafka was a prolific and consummate epistolary suitor — to the unhappily married Milena Jesenská from Merano in northern Italy where he was taking a further rest cure. He had been impressed by her translation of "The Stoker" into Czech and, when he met her after an intense correspondence, he was not less impressed by the woman. The romance flamed — Kafka's metaphor — but in the end the tormented Milena would not leave her husband, and Kafka came to the insight that his relationship with her had nowhere to go. But Kafka had somewhere to go: almost continually on sick leave, he was medically remanded now to a tuberculosis clinic and sanatorium at Matliary in the mountains of Slovakia. This was toward the end of a period during which he had written a number of short tales and parables typified by "The Top."

After some eight months' treatment and recuperation at Matliary, where he could not but understand the seriousness of his illness, he returned to Prague and to work at the Workers' Accident Insurance Institute. By October, his health again deteriorating, he was once more on a three months' sick leave. It was probably at the juncture between this sick leave and its renewal, in early 1922, that he began writing the novel *The Castle*. He had already informed Max Brod that he would request that all of his unpublished work — his novels and many of his shorter works — be destroyed after his death. The most recent shorter works included "A Hunger Artist," which had been published in a periodical, as well as "Advocates," "Investigations of a Dog," "Give It Up!" and "On Parables."

There were no more renewals of Kafka's sick leaves; it

would have been pointless to expect that he would ever be able to return to work. In June 1922 he retired, began drawing a pension, and went to live with his sister Ottla in Planá in southern Bohemia. There he worked on *The Castle* until he returned to Prague several months later. On a vacation the following summer with his sister Elli and her family on the Baltic coast he met a young Jewish girl, Dora Dymant, adept at Hebrew, from a Hasidic family. She seemed to supply the want of serious Judaism that Kafka had felt, as the product of a basically assimilationist culture.

He lived with Dora Dymant in Berlin, and she went with him in the spring of 1924 to Austria. He died of tuberculosis of the larynx at Kierling Sanatorium near Klosterneuburg on June 3, 1924. He was buried on June 11 in Prague's Jewish Cemetery. Max Brod gave a funeral speech and Dora Dymant, distraught, threw herself on the grave. Kafka's father turned away. During the last year of his life, Kafka wrote three stories that were published, along with "A Hunger Artist" from 1922, in the year of his death: "A Little Woman," "The Burrow," and "Josephine the Singer, or the Mouse Folk."

1

Early Prose:
Description of a Struggle,
"Wedding Preparations in the
Country," "The Judgment"

Kafka's earliest fiction, *Description of a Struggle,* was not written to be published. Although Kafka the law student, in 1904 and 1905, was moving in a circle of friends, including Max Brod, who read to each other from their own literary works in progress, he did not reveal that he was himself writing fiction. There is a certain irony — Kafka's sense of humor was one to savor it — that his fiction was thus more private as well as more self-revealing than his letters, which were, after all, destined for the eyes of his correspondents.

Evidently meant to be carried forward to novel length, *Description of a Struggle* was never completed. Its loose, episodic structure predicts the structure of Kafka's later novels, certainly in the form in which they have come down to us. It consists essentially of a dialogue between the narrating "I," a young man engaged to be married, and an interlocutor who is a bachelor — both transparent projections of Kafka himself — as they hike in Prague and environs on a clear, freezing February night. At one point the narrator casually orders his interlocutor to commit suicide. Also of thematic

importance is the engaged young artist's — he is an artist —
psychological (and physical) discomfort under the spell of his
bachelor acquaintance. Within this accommodating if chilly
framework is told, among others, the tale, "Conversation
with the Supplicant," which was extracted about four years
later and, with Brod's encouragement, published in the
Munich literary magazine, *Hyperion.*

The supplicant, who is the narrator of the encapsulated
tale, is in fact a romantic supplicant, extremely awkward and
self-conscious in making party conversation with a girl. He
insists on playing the piano, which, however, he does not
know how to do — although the girl and the other guests act
as if he had just played excellently. Kafka's awkward fictional
persona is concerned with believing that he is not awkward — why, after all, can't he just as well be one of the
graceful people? The tale ends with his departure from the
party — in someone else's overcoat, into which he has been
helped by the host. Just as in Kafka's mature works, so in this
early piece there is a juxtaposition of reality and fantasy, a
reflective, inhibiting self-consciousness and an erotic allu-
siveness.

The "struggle" in *Description of a Struggle* is pretty
clearly the struggle of the young engaged artist with himself
and, it may be inferred, the home environment that fights
his perceptions and his work as an artist. Although Kakfa
does not eschew fantasizing foreign locales, he is mostly
content to draw on Prague or the countryside about Prague
— as he was to continue to do. The episodic structure will
continue to characterize his longer works. While the style is
hardly that of the average law student, it is not yet the pol-
ished style that he was to command in his prime.

Episodic structure is certainly characteristic of "Wedding Preparations in the Country," which followed within
four years — and was likewise never to be completed. It was
similarly written — in three versions — primarily for himself,

although by now he was allowing Brod to look in on what he was writing. The writing of "Wedding Preparations" antedated by five years his meeting Felice Bauer. But already one can divine, without too much reliance on hindsight, that the first-person narrator is less than wildly enthusiastic about his trip to the countryside to see Betty and be introduced around as her fiancé.

As customary with Kafka's "I" narrators, Eduard Raban is a persona of Kafka himself. Even Raban's name is a cryptogram of the name Kafka, if not quite so instantly revealing as the nomenclature of some of his later fictional characters. In the case of Kafka-Raban each syllable of a two-syllable name is based on the vowel *a*.

Eduard Raban is an exhausted thirty-year-old Prague businessman—what Kafka was to become—who has committed himself to come visit Betty and her mother in the country. His thematic hesitation about the trip is revealed in his dour perceptions as well as in not especially well-motivated conversations. Serving the theme are the motifs of unseasonal rain—shop lights on at 4:30—the physical discomfort of travel, his yearning to return to the city, the dark, desolate, uncanny atmosphere of the countryside, and his suspiciousness about the people he is thrown into contact with on his lonely arrival. The arrival in the country is as far as any of the versions go. The reader never meets Betty, but it is clear that she has a fiancé whose love is most problematic.

Possibly more than on the mere basis of its intrinsic merit, "Wedding Preparations" is of interest because it incorporates, in inchoate but identifiable form, certain features that will reappear significantly in Kafka's mature prose. There is a quester, Raban, on a somewhat unfocused mission, which remains uncompleted. He is a tormented quester, uncertain of his role, ambiguous in the pursuit of his ambiguous mission. The structure is episodic. Irony is pervasive; for instance, the unrelenting, inhibiting, unseasonal rain in the first half of June—the month for marriages.

The motif of the double, or the split projection of the narrator, already present in *Description of a Struggle*, is here implied, not without irony, in the reluctant Raban's suggestion that it isn't really necessary for him to travel to the country, that he is just sending his clothed body. This lends ironic substance to the accumulating indication that most of the time his mind is in comfortable Prague while his body is suffering the discomforts of travel and rurality. And not merely in comfortable Prague, but in bed in comfortable Prague. There follows a scene foretelling the infamous transformation of a man into an insect in *The Metamorphosis*. Raban, though he has taken on the form of a beetle, has not actually become a bug but has split himself and identifies part of himself with a bug: "As I lie in bed I assume the shape of a big beetle, a stag beetle or a cockchafer, I think. . . . Then I would pretend it was a matter of hibernating, and I would press my little legs to my bulging belly. And I would whisper a few words, instructions to my sad body, which stands close beside me, bent."[1]

"The Judgment" is generally considered to be Kafka's breakthrough to truly successful fiction. Not least, by himself: though as a rule anything but sanguine about his own writing, he regarded and continued to regard "The Judgment" as a finished piece of writing—in both senses of the adjective. All the same, his critical hints reveal a certain bafflement as to what he was about. On his own word, the story is not at all the one he had in mind to write when he sat down at his desk at 10 o'clock on the evening of September 22, 1912. He wrote steadily, though apparently not rapidly, and by 6 in the morning "The Judgment," a story some twelve pages in length, was completed, and he was more than satisfied. It was published in a new yearbook of Brod's in 1913 and separately in 1916 and 1920. Although, like

Kafka's even earlier fiction, it anticipates his later works both thematically and stylistically, Kafka never included it with the later works that he condemned to destruction.

While "The Judgment" does represent a breakthrough and while it clearly connects with his subsequent writing, it bears comparison also with *Description of a Struggle* and "Wedding Preparations in the Country." In the former it will be recalled that the frame story consisted of a dialogue between the artist engaged to be married and a bachelor under whose influence the artist suffers serious distress. In "Wedding Preparations" it is the titular-thematic import that is to be kept in mind. Biographically as well as fictionally — that is, its contents — "The Judgment" is also in a sense a wedding preparation. For Kafka wrote it within weeks of his initial engagement to Felice Bauer, to whom it was dedicated. The name of the recently engaged heroine of the story, Frieda Brandenfeld, contains the same initials, F. B., as Felice Bauer, whose hometown, Berlin, was the capital of the historic province of Brandenburg. The Georg of the story is of course Franz — the same number of letters in the name, as Kafka points out. The fictional Georg's surname is Bendemann, the distinguishing part of which, Bende-, is a cryptogram for the name Kafka; as Kafka explains, it contains the same consonant/vowel pattern as his own surname. It is even, one might add, a cryptogram for a bound, a tied, an engaged Kafka if one applies enough first-level Indo-European etymologizing — of which Kakfa had a good awareness — to recognize *bende-* as a variant of the root of the German verb *binden*, meaning "to tie, to bind."

In the first part of the story Georg, a prosperous young businessman, has just finished writing a long letter to a friend in Russia, in St. Petersburg (Leningrad). The chief content of the letter is the hitherto withheld news that Georg has become engaged to one Frieda Brandenfeld, a young woman unknown to the bachelor friend in Petersburg. It is she, indeed, who has compelled Georg to inform his friend. The writing of the letter occasions a retrospective on Georg's circumstances, economic as well as personal. The former are most prosperous — in contrast to the friend's lot in Petersburg. In fact, Georg has practically taken over the family firm, guiding it to a dazzling prosperity and leaving his widowed father, with whom he shares a household, excluded from any effective role in the business.

The second part of the story finds Georg seeking out his father in the back room to report that he has finally written to Petersburg with the news of his engagement, and to seek paternal approval of his having done so. Confronting his father, Georg becomes aware that he has been neglecting the old man — who, however, is spirited — or forgetful, or sly — enough to imply that Georg has no friend in Petersburg, finally dismissing the very possibility as an utter joke. Georg, ever more aware of his neglect, becomes ever more solicitous, carrying the feeble old man to bed and tucking him in, covering him up well.

Too well, in fact. The old man rises up powerfully, reasserting himself. He proclaims that *he* is in touch with the friend in Russia (who then does exist after all), who thus already knows of Georg's engagement. The friend would be a son after his own heart. And he, the father, knows why his son is getting married: because his fiancée lifted her skirts. Georg, taken aback by the dynamic revival of his eclipsed and neglected father, resorts to invective: "You comedian." His father accepts this role — what else is left for a neglected widower? And in turn accuses Georg of immaturity — at least until his mother's death two years ago — and of overweening egocentricity, of being "a devilish human being." Then he utters his condemnation, the sentence, the judgment, from which the story takes its title: "I sentence you now to death by drowning!"[2]

Georg, as though urged by some metaphysical force,

rushes down the stairs, across the street, onto the bridge (at which he had been gazing in a mellow mood at the story's outset), and over the railing into the water as a bus passes that would cover the noise of his fall. His final words he calls out in a low voice as he lets himself drop: "Dear parents, I have always loved you, all the same."[3]

A casual reader might at first be inclined to suppose that the participants in such goings-on are quite irrational, perhaps insane, or that the whole is actually a nightmare. Though not without its dreamlike aspects — for example, the spectacular resurgence of Georg's father's strength, his dancing on the bed — the story contains too much inner logic for it to be considered a dream from beginning to end. Nor is there any narrative frame to suggest that it is a dream. It is not a real world either, although the descriptions — before the antic climax and ending — are real enough, as, for example, the description of the Petersburg friend's situation there, in effect all alone in a vast and inhospitable Russia. (The country itself, however realistically described, seems nonetheless to be predominantly a metaphor as I will shortly come to consider.) The world of the story, neither dream nor real, seems to be above all a world that elucidates — and is elucidated by — the personal relationships. And the relationships themselves are, as one might already have supposed from Kafka's earlier writing, connected to his own painful personal situation. Painful, but not without the possibility of being seen ironically by the person in the center, that is, by the writer himself.

From Kafka's diary entries, not to mention the cryptogrammic nature of the names of his fictional characters, the reader is amply justified in associating the (letter-)writer Georg Bendemann with the writer Franz Kafka, and the fictional fiancée Frieda Brandenfeld with the real-life fiancée Felice Bauer. If one visualizes triangles of personal relationships, the senior Bendemann of the fiction is to be associated with the redoubtable Hermann Kafka. In Georg's bachelor friend in Russia one may wish to recognize Kafka's alter ego, as in the early narrative pieces. The friend's position in the fictional triangle would then be coincident with Georg's—or it may be preferable to think of him as at some remove, isolated, cut off in the desolate wilds of Russia.

It is the interrelation of the characters that provides the dynamics of the story. One notes the obvious fact that neither Frieda Brandenfeld nor the friend in Russia is present in person: their circumstances, their actions, their attitudes are reported chiefly by Georg, to a lesser extent—and conflictingly—by his father. The narrative point of view is that of Georg, the focus of a presumably omniscient author who, however—this becomes the characteristic narrative style in Kafka's works—fails to impart to the reader any very large portion of his omniscience. The narration is tortuous. The reader has to work, to speculate, to search for structures beyond the interactions of the characters, although suggested by those interactions.

It is conceptually economical to suggest that an unresolved Oedipal relationship determines the relationship of Georg and his father. Evidently, the father had held the upper hand, the weight of power, psychological power as well as power in the family firm, for as long as his wife, Georg's mother, lived, that is, until two years ago. Georg was apparently—the reader may infer pretextual status from hints in the text—a dutiful son, younger then and diligent and attentive. If he had aspirations or tendencies to become a loner, a writer (other than of letters) rather than a functionary in the family firm, they were suppressed. If he had girlfriends—the text is silent here—certainly no previous relationship had become so serious as to lead to plans for marriage.

But now . . . ! Georg is engaged, he is powerful, he has taken over the direction of the company, he has relegated his father to the dark back room, he reads the newspaper in preference to talking with him, he has ignored the fact that his father's personal habits have become untidy, he—in a spasm of belated filial awareness—will arrange for the doctor to give the old man a checkup. Anxiously, because he cannot refuse the insistence of his fiancée that he write, he will go to the back room to seek the old man's approval, after the fact, of what he has written, but not yet mailed, to his friend in Russia about his plans to marry.

However, in the course of that interview—at the outset of which Georg already feels helpless and at the end of which he goes to pieces—the roles are reversed; the father, likened to a giant, reasserts his dominance in the most definitive way. The turning point is the play on the concept of covering up—in Georg's mind, at least on the surface, snugly covering up the old man in bed, in the old man's mind, however, being covered up metaphorically, as in being relegated to negligence, or to a grave. He springs up, standing on the bed, flinging blankets and insults with equal force—a grotesque, nightmarish spectacle. The spectacle ends only with Georg's unreluctant compliance with the pronouncement of the paternal judgment: death by drowning. The judgment of the father—note well—who has proclaimed himself the "representative" of the friend in Russia, the friend who constituted in Kafka's own view "the greatest bond" between Georg and his father. If the friend as Georg's alter ego symbolizes aloneness, if not perhaps also the aloneness of the artist, then Georg's predisposition to aloneness—to being an artist?—is thereby triumphing over Georg's recent emergence as a successful businessman making his way into society, an entry to be reinforced by his presumable marriage to Frieda Brandenfeld, who is introduced to the reader not as a lovable girl but—can it be insignificant?—as "a girl from a well-to-do family."

It may be helpful to examine the quality of the reader's

sympathy with Georg. It derives chiefly from his carrying out his father's grotesque — it seems almost whimsical — condemnation. But a rereading — always a good idea with the works of Kafka — of the first part of the story may lead one to see in Georg a not particularly admirable young man. The principal source for this negative feeling lies in the tone of his letter and of his past letters to his friend in Petersburg. Less than straightforward, when not downright dishonest, the present letter is fundamentally manipulative. Does or doesn't Georg want his friend to come to his wedding? For all of Georg's flowery pretense of regard for feelings, it would be an imperceptive friend who would accept such an invitation as Georg insincerely extends.

With his father as well Georg has been manipulative — if one can countenance the idea of a neglectful manipulation. In any event, the proposed rehabilitation of filial duty is manipulative in the face of it. For example, Georg cannot seem to abide the old man's preference for a closed window in warm weather — at least Georg *says* it's warm. Nor for eating sparingly. Nor, one may infer, for a meaningful role in his own business firm. The problem for Georg is that the old man, unlike his Russian friend and unlike his fiancée, is present in the here and now, and he reacts.

He overreacts, he reacts nightmarishly. Much of the scene in the dark back bedroom is of antic, comic grotesqueness. The old man standing on the bed, kicking his legs, "radiant with insight" into Georg's purportedly merely sexual reason for marrying. Georg in a corner, jockeying for maximum distance from the reinvigorated old man. (As on the stage, distance, its decrease, its increase, is important.) Georg acquiesces in his father's coarse annihilation of Frieda Brandenfeld. Georg surrenders her, as he surrenders his friendship with the friend in Petersburg. All he can do is mock his father, call him a comedian, a designation the father gladly and not illogically accepts. Surrender here, surrender there — does the reader doubt that Georg will also surrender his own life and his writing (the unsent letter still in his pocket)?

In contrast to the sober first part, the second part of "The Judgment" is not only grotesque, but even surreal and nightmarish. Which is not to say that it is completely alogical in the fashion of a dream; the overall logic is firm throughout the grotesquerie — including the paternal judgment and Georg's compliance. And yet the superior logic in underlain by details of dream logic, in which wish is tantamount to fact, in which juxtaposition suffices as cause and effect. Thus there is something like twofold cause for anticipating Georg's meek acceptance of the murderous caprice of his father. Shortly before, while his father had been cavorting madly on the bed after having declared himself to be the representative of the friend in Russia, Georg allowed himself the parricidal speculation on what it would be like if his father should topple, and smash himself. His father doesn't topple, and he does pronounce Georg's anathema, which Georg — guilty Georg — is prepared to take quite literally.

2

The Metamorphosis, "The Stoker"

Kafka wrote *The Metamorphosis* in November and December 1912, thus within two or three months of the night in September when he wrote "The Judgment" in a single sitting. *The Metamorphosis* took a little longer, three weeks. The composition, moreover, was interrupted by the necessity of superintending the family-owned asbestos factory for two weeks while the superintendent was on a business trip. To this rankling interruption, added to his duties in the insurance office, Kafka attributed at least some of his dissatisfaction with the novella recorded in his diary in late 1913 and early 1914. Although he had earlier expressed satisfaction with the story, a year later he found it to be fundamentally—or almost fundamentally—flawed. He branded the ending as "unreadable." It seems a curious if authentic judgment on a novella that has become one of the most widely read and discussed works of twentieth-century literature, a comic tragedy of modern man's isolation, alienation, inadequacy, and guilt.

Despite Kafka's insistence that the protagonist Gregor Samsa "is not merely Kafka and nothing else,"[1] the fictional surname is obviously a cryptogram—Kafka himself notes the similarity—of the author's surname.[2] It is indeed a more precise cryptogram, consonant for consonant, vowel for vowel, than that borne by Raban in "Wedding Preparations in the Country," with whom Gregor shares also the distinction of turning into an insect. In Gregor's case the metamorphosis is different in that it is, first unwilled, second definitive, and third total—that is, there is no split of Gregor's being once he becomes a bug. In short, Gregor Samsa, a traveling salesman who by dint of exhausting labor has been supporting his parents and his sister, awakes one rainy morning after troubled dreams to find himself transformed into a monstrous bug, evidently a beetle or much like a beetle. Unable to go to work, he is virtually held prisoner by his family, while his formerly idle father, with new vigor, resumes work. The loathsome bug is not only held prisoner, kept in his room as much as possible, but he is also violently persecuted by his father. His mother ineffectually pleads for Gregor, and his sister feeds—or tries to feed—her metamorphosed brother. But Gregor fails to find satisfaction or nourishment in the fresh food that she at first places before him. Alternately ignored and persecuted, he gradually starves and dies—to the resurgent joy of his family.

The Metamorphosis, formally structured, has no sense of the incompleteness that marks much of Kafka's fiction—not only the novels. It has three Roman-numbered sections, the latter two each reiterating their predecessors, yet emphasizing and adding as well, and each section ending with its own climax. In the first section when Gregor, already an insect as the story opens, ventures from his bedroom, he is repelled by his enraged father. In the second section, now more reconciled to his insect predicament—preferring, for example, to eat rotten food rather than fresh milk—he is again driven out of the living room by his father and back to his bedroom. From this foray he receives the possibly fatal apple—thrown by his father—lodged in his back. In the third section, attracted as a nonhuman by the spirit emanating from his sister's violin-playing, he is once more driven back to his room where, without his actively willing it, death soon follows — whether brought about by the apple or gradual starvation.

The reader is correct in regarding the father-son relationship — as in "The Judgment" — as basic to *The Metamorphosis.* Indeed it was at one point Kafka's desire to publish these two thematically related novellas, together with "The Stoker," in a single volume under the suggestive title, *Sons.* A more specifically appropriate title would have been "The Estranged Son." But in *The Metamorphosis* Kafka has a much firmer artistic grip both on his estrangement and on his fictional alter ego. That is, he achieves a bit of artistic distance from the unfortunate Gregor Samsa — distance perhaps compelled by the inevitable humor, as well as horror, involved in causing his alter ego to turn into a monstrous bug. In the event, his view of the bug is from the outside and his sympathy is tempered with humor; for example, the bug delights in devouring a piece of cheese that Gregor in human form just two days ago had pronounced inedible.

Conceivably, it is tempting to maintain that Gregor as insect is a delusion on the part of Gregor, that he remains human but imagines himself an insect. Kafka seems to provide little leeway, however, for such an interpretation, declaring forthrightly at the outset of the second paragraph, "It was no dream."[3] Still, it is a valid critical insight that Gregor, as a loathsome insect, has become that which he was made to feel by his family, especially by his father; but also by his employer, by his life as a traveling salesman, by — there is more than ample textual warrant — his society, that is, by exploitive, rapacious, dehumanizing, capitalistic industrial society. His metamorphosis is already an accomplished fact before the story opens. Kafka gives it to the reader whole on the first page and thereafter calmly insists on its reality. Although the reader knows that such a transformation is impossible, he or she probably has been induced by Kafka's skillful dissociation to suspend disbelief.

The kind of bug that Gregor has changed into has excit-
ed a bit of speculation. Raban, in "Wedding Preparations in
the Country," was (partly) a beetle, in German, *Käfer*. This
seems to have led a number of critics to assume that Gregor
Samsa was likewise a beetle, an assumption comfortably reinforced by the fact that the cleaning woman employed by
the Samsas refers to their metamorphosed son as an "old
dung beetle." But to take the coarse and comic cleaning
woman's taxonomic view in preference to that of the dispas-
sionate and generally well-informed narrator seems not especially well advised. The narrator, who in Kafka's fiction is
pretty obviously Kafka himself, calls the creature *ein unge-
heueres Ungeziefer*, of which the noun, *Ungeziefer*, is not
very specific at all, something like English "vermin," which
some translators prefer to "insect" or "bug." *Ungeheuer(es)*
means "monstrous."

It is probably revealing that Kafka uses a noun that
inhibits a clear visual image of the bug. Revealing, that is, of
the irrelevance of the exact taxonomy of the insect. When
Kafka's publisher commissioned an illustration by Ottomar
Starke for the story, Kafka inveighed against any depiction of
the insect itself: "The insect itself cannot be drawn."[4] His
wish evidently was heeded; Starke drew a human figure.
Later artists, even from the circle of Kafka's friends and
admirers, were not daunted—for example, Otto Coester in
his folio volume, *Proměna, šestero konfiguracíi k stejno-
jmenné povídce Frant. Kafky* (*Metamorphosis, Six Illustrations to the Story of the Same Name by Franz Kafka*).[5] The
most detailed of Coester's illustrations is of an indetermi-
nate scaly bug measuring perhaps two by three feet, with an
array of legs that are highly detailed, irregular, and quasi-
human. Among the scales on the lower part of the body is
the design of a man's face—the face of the father, as one
sees from the other illustrations.

Of course, the father is the focus of Gregor's alienation—the perpetrator of assaults on him, the thrower of the apple that seems to be at least in part responsible for Gregor's death. It is the father who in the first place is responsible for Gregor's wage-slavery to his pitiless employer, for Gregor's wretched existence as a traveling salesman. For the collapse of his father's business and the resulting debt had obliged Gregor to undertake the support of the family. He did so capably, gradually also working off the debt (his employer was also his father's creditor). But at what a personal cost! No job could have been more demanding, more dehumanizing. And while his father became a layabout, lounging around the flat all day long in his dressing gown, unable to rise in greeting when Gregor returned from a wearying day, Gregor had effectively, unthinkingly supplanted the old man and himself taken over the role of paterfamilias.

Coincident with Gregor's metamorphosis into a bug is the transformation of his prematurely retired father into an active, proud breadwinner for his family. Almost forced by circumstance, Gregor had encroached on this paternal preserve—now reclaimed by the pater redivivus (whom the reader compares with the father rampant in "The Judgment"). The father's new position is that of a bank messenger. Even at home he proudly wears the smart blue uniform of his new calling, complete with gold buttons. While Gregor, of course, wears the less-splendid raiment of a repulsive insect—although ironically this may well cover a creature in the process of becoming more human, psychologically speaking, than when he was an automaton-employee.

As a sensitive bug, Gregor has to witness the scene that above all he would rather not see; the father in perfect sexual union with his wife (preceded by a comic tableau vivant of one petticoat after another falling down as the mother, stumbling, hurls herself on the father). The Oedipal component, a given in Kafka's fiction, here finds simultaneously traumatizing, poignant, and comic expression—reflecting the unusual distancing that Kafka has managed to attain in *The Metamorphosis.*

Together with the father's sharp uniform and revived sexual energy goes his insistence on remaining in his seat of power in the living room even when so drunken with sleep that the women of the household must drag and propel him to bed. Sartorially (though the continually worn uniform was picking up grease spots), sexually, physically renascent, he also resumes his management of the family purse—which, thanks to Gregor's former efforts as well as to a reserve fund somehow salvaged from the collapse of the business, is in fact in rather good shape. The reader does not miss the irony in this: the presumably ruinous state of the family finances was after all the reason Gregor had enslaved himself to his employer and become subject to the dehumanization that took literal shape in his transformation into a bug. The elder Samsa fully reasserts his domestic authority by summarily evicting the three boarders who had been usurping the power in the flat, relegating the Samsas to the kitchen to eat their meals. Samsa senior can even afford a little indulgence toward the imprisoned Gregor: he allows the door to Gregor's bedroom to be left ajar so that Gregor might have the solace of watching and listening to his family around the lamp-lit table.

The reestablishment of bourgeois family hegemony under the aegis of the father is signaled by Kafka's nomenclature. Suddenly, well toward the end of part III, on the cleaning woman's shouted report that the insect that was Gregor was quite dead, the father and mother, sitting up in bed, are given back their bourgeois designation: Mr. and Mrs. Samsa. As that unadmirable dual entity they will shortly—after Gregor's body, flat and dry, is swept away—perceive that their daughter Grete is blossoming and shapely. In a word, Grete is highly marriageable, a condition not without its advantage to Mr. and Mrs. Samsa. From an ironic and antibourgeois point of view it could be said that, having sacrificed Gregor to the system, they are quite prepared to do the same – if in a different way – to Grete.

Grete, one recalls, was the only family member with whom the metamorphosed Gregor had any rapport – and that rapport did not survive the impact of disparity, nor, somewhat more inferentially, her emergence from ebullient girlhood to a more mature awareness of the nature and realities of her world. At first Grete tried conscientiously to do what she could for Gregor: to find out what he would eat, to make him feel comfortable, to anticipate his wishes. She was the family expert on Gregor, his representative, as best she could be, to their uncomprehending mother and their antagonistic and resurgent father. But then she too, burdened by an impossible charge in dealing with the unkown, undergoes, at about sixteen years of age, her own metamorphosis: into a practical-minded young woman who would honor the memory of her brother but who would at the same time want to get rid of the noisome bug that inhabits his room.

The violin-playing episode – and Gregor's reaction to it – is the climax and the symbol of Grete's metamorphosis. The boarders appear to be interested in hearing her play further; an impromptu recital is arranged. Despite her beautiful, soulful playing, however, they become bored and irritated. Not so Gregor, who, profoundly affected, "as if the way were opening before him to the unknown nourishment he craved,"[6] crawls forward. No one here appreciates her playing, he reflects, as he would appreciate it if she would come into his room with her violin; he would never let her out, but in any case she would stay of her own free will.

Thus the would-be enlistment of Grete in Gregor's longing for otherwordly nourishment, now more spiritual than alimentary. Gregor certifies the spirituality by reflecting further that only as an insect (an insect unburdened of human materialism) has he been able to be at one with beautiful music—when he was a human being it had meant nothing to him. The reader, however, will also have sensed in Gregor's reflections and fantasies about his sister an incestuous desire. Latent it had doubtless been, while he was in human form; as the music frees his spiritual desire, so also it releases a less spiritual desire.

How long does Grete play to this desire, does she even divine it? One cannot be at all certain. The recital ends when the middle roomer descries Gregor's advance, when the roomers demand explanations; for a while Grete's eyes continue to follow the score after she has stopped playing. Laying the violin in her mother's lap while the roomers announce their intention of leaving "in view of the disgusting conditions," she hastens into their room and in a skillfully managed flurry of pillows and blankets makes their beds and slips out. Thus is symbolized, as the violin slips onto the floor with a reverberating clang, her rejection of Gregor, of her rapport with Gregor, of, possibly, her uncritical adolescence, and on the other hand her acceptance of her domestic, adult function in the real world—her metamorphosis. It is at this point that she dissociates the name of her brother from the insect: "We must try to get rid of it." And later: "It has to go."[7] Gregor is no longer "he," but "it," although some English versions fail to make this important distinction. And as its sister locks it up in Gregor's room, its end is near. Its last glance, on being forced back into its room, is at its mother—now fast asleep after the tumultuous scene.

While Gregor both early and late yearns for his mother, and she after his initial imprisonment began fairly soon to want to visit him, there is no metamorphosis in her case. She remains a somewhat intermediate character: less hostile than the father, not without an occasional flash of insight superior to the sister's, but on the whole unsure of herself, overexcited (but who wouldn't be?), given to asthmatic seizure, anxious to indulge and please her husband—not far from a caricature of the bourgeois housewife that she has been and will be again when the Samsas, prosperous, if fewer in number, find a smaller, more advantageously located apartment. As caricature the mother is outshone only by the bawling cleaning woman with an ostrich feather in her hat, who gleefully reports that she has performed the function of disposing of Gregor's dessicated body. For her, never having known Gregor before his metamorphosis, things are simpler: "it" has always been an "it."

The reader, like the cleaning woman, need perhaps not be unduly grieved at Gregor's death — though for a different reason, namely that of insight. Gregor was unsuited for, dissatisfied with, the normal if extremely burdensome existence that he was obliged to be a part of. Of course, that existence was paradoxical — and hardly happy. But Gregor is incapable of articulating his desire for a different nourishment, and this is as true figuratively as it is literally. He accordingly comes to see that he must disappear. With an apple — fruit of knowledge — lodged immovably and painfully but perhaps not mortally on his back, he dries up from a not very forcefully willed self-starvation.

Dawn is beginning to lighten the world outside his window as his head sinks to the floor of its own accord and he breathes his last. Penultimate illumination through a window occurs as more than one Kafka hero expires. Some take this as a sign of eschatological hope. Max Brod in particular likes to see such hope in Kafka. Others prefer to see a light through a window, or maybe through a doorway, as a dimension of irony. In Kafka's concept the same light could very well represent at once both hope *and* irony.

"The Stoker," which became the first chapter of the novel *Amerika*, was originally published separately (and is still often published separately). It appeared in May 1913 as part of the new magazine, *Der jüngste Tag* (Doomsday), launched by

Kafka's publisher-friend Kurt Wolff. Whereas Kafka by that time abhorred his five hundred remaining pages of the would-be novel, *Amerika*, he was satisfied with the first chapter, even while recognizing that it was not complete in itself.

"The Stoker" and practically the whole of *Amerika* were written during the same period as "The Judgment" and *The Metamorphosis*. Yet in *Amerika* Kafka was in effect backing away from his other writing by employing many of the conventions of nineteenth-century realistic fiction, a mode that he detested and a relapse that he could not countenance in himself. Thus it was that he made no attempt to publish the novel but submitted for publication only "The Stoker," which in his view escaped the opprobrious mode of the longer work.

While one proceeds cautiously in accepting *all* of Kafka's critical dicta — he could be neurotically self-rejecting — in this case his estimate of the relative integrity of the story "The Stoker" and the novel *Amerika* is perhaps close to the mark. Like "The Judgment" and, perhaps to a lesser — or different — degree, *The Metamorphosis*, "The Stoker" begins in an essentially realistic direction but soon turns in the direction of something like surrealism or at least of realism operating under conditions of dream-logic. Thus the reader encounters Karl Rossmann, a fifteen- or sixteen-year-old immigrant from Prague, on the deck of a Hamburg-American steamer as it enters New York harbor. Suddenly recalling that he has left his umbrella in steerage, he precipitately leaves his footlocker with all his possessions — and mementos of his former life — in the charge of a stranger and sets off between decks to retrieve his umbrella.

Promptly losing his way in an unfamiliar part of the ship, he blunders into the quarters of a giant stoker, with whom he feels a sudden and uncritical sympathy. With the stoker he makes his way to the captain's stateroom to plead, very eloquently, the stoker's grievance against his immediate superior. There, in the company of an assortment of dignitaries from on board and from the harbor authority—at the final stage of a five-day crossing, the captain really has more pressing concerns than petty rivalries among the crew—Karl is recognized by his long-lost wealthy uncle, who takes him ashore to his own splendid house. As he had abandoned his footlocker with scarcely a thought, Karl now abandons— forced by the situation, it is true—the stoker and the stoker's case—which may well prove to be a noncase.

Publicizing the facts of the stoker's case reveals a gap between the presumed (by Karl) reality and the actual state of things. The complaint boils down to the impression by the stoker that he is the victim of anti-German prejudice on the part of his superior, a Rumanian named Schubal. Schubal's rebuttal as well, however, though couched in effective bureaucratic language, is shot through with inconsistency and perhaps lies and manipulation.

The piecemeal revelation of Karl's plight during the bizarre tribunal in the captain's quarters suggests as well that some of the reader's early impressions from the story lack correspondence with reality. For example, in the very first line Kafka's narrator refers to Karl's "poor parents." Only gradually does one come to recognize the reality that they are not poor at all, neither as to financial resources nor as to meriting any sort of claim to sympathy. Put more broadly, Karl lacks a correspondence with the external reality of the world. He has been arbitrarily severed, thanks to his scandalously cruel parents, from the old world that he knows; and of the new world he knows nothing—perhaps his fear of it is suggested by his initial haste to return to the bowels of the ship in search of his umbrella.

In similar fashion his rescuer, Uncle Jacob, gives out a romanticized cliché version of Karl's seduction by the thirty-five-year-old family cook—whom Karl impregnated—which

Karl is constrained to correct publicly. He neither had nor has any feeling for her, even if she has been thoughtful enough — or self-interested enough (she named the baby Jacob) — to fully inform Uncle Jacob by letter of Karl's impending arrival. It is of course owing to the mésalliance with the cook that Karl's "poor" parents kick him out of the house, out of town, in fact off the old continent, away from everything familiar, and consign him alone and unaided — except for the cook's letter — to the alien mercies of the new continent.

And yet, in his profound naïveté, Karl accepts all this with equanimity and apparently unblemished devotion, speculating fondly how he would rise in his parents' esteem if they could only see him valiantly pleading the cause of justice for his sudden friend, the stoker. The significance of the instinctive rapport with the stoker lies in the stoker's symbolizing the German world that for Karl is forever lost. Just how totally lost is confirmed by the self-conscious Americanism of his guardian-to-be, Uncle Jacob, the very model of exploitative capitalistic endeavor.

The reader may detect a less-savory component in Karl's presumable naïveté, and it too is on view in his eloquent if unsuccessful espousal of the stoker's cause. It is egotism. Karl glories in the ego-satisfaction provided by his advocacy of the stoker. He revels in fantasizing a joint physical assault on their adversary, Schubal. And when one reflects, it *would* require no small ego-strength for a boy of fifteen or sixteen, having been unceremoniously shunted across the ocean forever, to still be interested in even the theoretical approbation of the parents who had thus disposed of him. It will be helpful to keep in mind Karl Rossmann's resilient ego when one follows him into the novel that Max Brod published after Kafka's death under the name *Amerika*, although Kafka's title had been *Lost without Trace*.

3

Amerika

Kafka's original title for the novel Max Brod published in 1927 under the name *Amerika* was *Der Verschollene*, which in English means *Lost without Trace*, or, more accurately if less concisely, *The Man Who Disappeared without a Trace* or *The Man Who Was Never Heard of Again*. If Kafka's title reflects Kafka's intention, as there is every reason to think it must, then clearly one should be cautious about subscribing, as more than an occasional critic does, to the notion that the novel contains an optimistic resolution — except in the most ironic, even parodistic sense.

Kafka's own condemnation of the novel seems to rest on two related particulars. While not abandoning the assumptions of dream-narrative (as distinct from mere dream) that typify, for example, "The Judgment" (at least to some degree) and *The Metamorphosis,* he here combined the dream mode with that of naturalism — a thoroughgoing, perhaps tendentious realism eclipsing by far the eclectic descriptions to be found in the earlier stories. And for Kafka naturalism, which with a capital N dominated German literature in the last decade of the nineteenth and the first years of the twentieth century, was the shallowest kind of writing.

Second, he perceived "The Stoker" as "a sheer imitation of Dickens, the projected novel [*Amerika*] even more so."[1] He knew Dickens's works well but had become disenchanted by Dickens's richness of characters, repetitiveness of incident, and what Kafka regarded as oversentimentality. That Dickens was able to transcend episodic structure and weave his characters and incidents into an embracing plot seems not to have inspired Kafka to do likewise — which amounts to a telling criticism of *Amerika,* although Kafka's self-criticism stopped short of that conclusion.

Kafka's literary judgments, as far as they go, are perhaps sounder than those of many an author, and one has to accord special weight to his verdict on his own work. In any case his own criticism seems to have become the basis of the standard critical opinion that *Amerika* is inferior to his later novels, *The Trial* and *The Castle* — if not simply an inferior novel. As a result *Amerika* has received far less serious critical attention than the later novels, much of it centering about an insistence on its uniqueness in the Kafka oeuvre.

It is not really that unique, though, if one discounts the fact that it takes place not in Prague — or at any rate in central Europe — but in the United States. Or, to put it more discerningly, ostensibly in the United States. For in spite of having drawn from sources relating to America, including Benjamin Franklin's autobiography, and his own notion that Americans were vitalistic and optimistic, Kafka did not transcend in *Amerika* — perhaps had no intention of transcending — the limitation of never having been there. His physical America, starting with the very seascape and landscape of New York, lacks verisimilitude and rather resembles Europe, both actual and futuristic. His essential America, on the other hand, its opulence side-by-side with grinding poverty, is of sufficient authenticity to make it a dynamic background to, or adversary of, the contemplative, quintessentially European middle-school pupil, Karl Rossmann. An adversary from which, however, Karl never learns.

Structurally, the novel consists of a number of episodes in which the innocent — but afflicted with existential guilt[2] — perfectionistic, sublimely egotistic Karl Rossmann is exploited, seduced, deceived, and insulted. In short, he is brought to one fall after another in an America that remains incomprehensible to him from beginning to end — even an apparently utopian end in which he suddenly is accorded acceptance. These episodes coincide with the seven chapters that follow "The Stoker," as arranged by Max Brod. Finally — though lacking in some American editions — there are two fragmentary chapters placed by Brod in an appendix. Narratively, they belong between the penultimate chapter and the final, utopian chapter.

Karl's Uncle Jacob, a powerful and influential father figure, does not exploit the youth in quite the same gross fashion as the later exploiters — although his emotional exploitation hardly lacks in cruelty. He offers Karl every material and social advantage that an immigrant boy could desire. But, characteristically more an apostle of presumed Americanism than many a native American, he obtrudes his materialistic, entrepreneurial point of view on Karl with remarkable insensitivity. As selfish emotionally as commercially, Jacob is unwilling to allow Karl any social latitude — perhaps, it is true, premature latitude — with his, Jacob's, small circle of business friends, Mr. Green and Mr. Pollunder. By impetuously — it seems almost whimsically — repudiating Karl Jacob deprives himself as well as Karl of any closeness that may have developed between uncle and nephew, even as he casts his nephew onto the streets of the overwhelming foreign country that is America.

If one thinks of Karl as the victim of a series of exploiters, then his initial exploiter was the Johanna Brummer — this was still in Europe, in his parents' home — who lovelessly seduced and had a child by him. The second was the stoker. The third is his Uncle Jacob. Or perhaps the third is Pollunder's daughter Klara, who attempts to seduce him, and the fourth is Uncle Jacob. The pattern of the novel and of Karl's life is in any case well established: exploitation, failed or

unauthentic rapport, banishment. Ever submissive, ever
hopeful but above all in America ever lacking the necessary
insight into the scheme of life, Karl takes it. He takes it
repeatedly, even resiliently, but the course of his life is inevitably downward.

On the streets after being forbidden ever to contact his
Uncle Jacob again, in fact on the road in the direction of a
city called Ramses, Karl falls in with a pair of vagabond
unemployed machinists named Delamarche and Robinson.
After suffering their insults and their plundering, he escapes
them, at least for a while, by taking refuge in the Hotel
Occidental where, through the good offices of the formerly
Viennese chief cook, he finds exploitative employment as an
elevator boy. From this post he is fired for first, deserting his
station for two minutes without authorization and second
for lodging Robinson, his unwanted and drunken road acquaintance, in Karl's dormitory in an innocent — but also self-
defensive — effort to get him out of management's sight.

Through the agency of Robinson and misapplied police
vigilance Karl is returned to the toils of the anarchistic Delamarche. Brutally he is forced to be Delamarche's servant in
the flat shared by Delamarche, his monstrously fat mistress,
Brunelda, and his companion and erstwhile servant, Robinson. Between this sorry exploitation and the Karl of the final
chapter, who finds unconditional acceptance as a technical
apprentice in the utopian Theater of Oklahoma, there is a
narrative gap. This gap is filled only partially by two fragmentary chapters that seem to reiterate only more convincingly Karl's degradation in the sexually charged Delamarche
menage and, finally, in conducting Brunelda to a whore-
house, with which Karl has some sort of flunky's job.

The pervasive motif of seduction may well serve as a
model of exploitation and fall in *Amerika,* and not only in
Amerika, which is not fundamentally different from the
Kafka oeuvre. Nor is the adduction of such a motif merely

capricious. The very first sentence of *Amerika* (thus of "The Stoker") begins as follows: "As Karl Rossmann, a poor boy of sixteen who had been packed off to America by his parents because a servant girl had seduced him and got herself a child by him. . . ."[3]

By virtue of its primacy, Karl's seduction is thus the "fundamental event" of the novel, as a perceptive German critic noted some two decades ago.[4] Thereafter follows his cruel expulsion by his parents, his fall from grace to an unknowable fate in America. That expulsion, replicated by the melancholy fate of the stoker — betrayed by the coquettish kitchen maid, Line, with whom he had a shipboard relationship — portends the recurrent motif sequence: seduction is followed by expulsion and fall. With each successive expulsion and fall Karl's situation and prospects deteriorate further. The reader will likely become convinced that in the end they are quite hopeless, unlikely to be restored under the auspices of the fantastic and probably parodistic Nature Theater of Oklahoma.

Of course, seductions of the sort first experienced by Karl at home were rites of passage in middle-class European homes with a teenage son and a maidservant. It has been suggested that the Kafka household was among them.[5] But none of this is very important from a structural point of view. What is important is that as a direct consequence of his seduction Karl is torn from his family — in itself not necessarily a bad thing — severed from his previous life and his prospects for life, and deposited into the maelstrom of America.

Temporarily redeemed from this expulsory trauma by the jealous beneficence of his Uncle Jacob, he is understandably shy of the hoydenish advances of Klara Pollunder at her father's Long Island estate — which is actually more like a European castle. Klara, already regularly sleeping with her fiancé Mack, is rather clearly aiming at some variety in the person of her father's overnight guest, Karl Rossmann. (Is it apprehensiveness of just such a development that decides Uncle Jacob against Karl's venture into a wider society?)

Karl is impressed by Klara's red lips (which remind him of her father's lips). He is not unwilling to accept her invitation to join her in her suite, not least to play the piano for her pleasure. On the other hand, he is neither pleased nor comfortable with her flirting nor with her tendency to take over as an assertive, even aggressive, hostess, to issue commands, to push and pull him around. The tussling takes on amorous overtones, with teasing and embracing: "It was easy enough to grip her in her tight dress."[6] Why is she sighing so, he wonders — it can't be hurting her that much — and by now they are calling each other by the intimate pronoun *du*. Forcing Karl onto the bed in his room, Klara challenges him to transfer activities to her room.

Klara strides about the room, "her skirt rustling about her legs; she seemed to pause for a long time by the window."[7] Her pausing by the window has quite as much erotic association as her skirt rustling about her legs. For several moments earlier the narrator had noted that the moonlight did not penetrate Karl's dark room. Now, a few minutes later, the reader infers that Klara, in her tight dress and with the moon as a backlight, is pausing at length at the window so that Karl can now appreciate the outline of her figure as he had earlier experienced the feel of it. Klara is far more seductive than the loathsomely fumbling Johanna Brummer. Karl, not without apprehension, is riding for another, and perhaps more melancholy, fall.

This time the word of his fall is conveyed in a letter from Uncle Jacob not to be opened before midnight — Kafka has adapted the Cinderella motif. Karl is expelled from the elite and comfortable ambience of his Uncle Jacob and his friends and into the criminal company of the proletarians

Robinson and Delamarche — "on the road," as Delamarche's very name reveals. And through them, or rather in flight from them, into the work force of the Hotel Occidental. Where, still in his submissive innocence and readiness to please, still exploitable, still in the state of guilt as such, he is awaited by another seduction — like that by Klara probably unconsummated — and another dreary fall: back down into the marginal criminal existence of Delamarche and Robinson. In the Hotel Occidental it is Therese Berchtold, the secretary-typist for Karl's protectress, the chief cook — it is Therese who is the almost-seductress.

Despite her shyness, it is Therese who invades Karl's makeshift bedroom. To be sure, she gives him, already undressed, ample opportunity to get beneath the covers. Karl confides to her that it would have been better if he had put his clothes back on before her visit. He fails to tell her that he doesn't even have a nightshirt on. Whatever Karl's innocence — and, one is persuaded, Therese's as well — enumeration of such details lends an intimate, not to say potentially suggestive, tone to the confidences of the pair.

Therese, confessing to being so alone in her life — in spite of her obviously friendly relationship with the chief cook — sits down so close to Karl that he feels compelled to move clear back to the wall. Mostly their conversation consists of Therese's imparting details about her career at the hotel and of her reiteration that she has no one to talk to. Crying, she presses her face into the bedclothes. Karl permits enough of his arm to emerge to stroke her arm consolingly. In departing she runs her hand gently over his blanket.

On only three occasions is Karl in Therese's room for a rather long time, longer than a few hours. It must have been on one of those occasions that she relates to him the central — but somehow oddly detached — socioeconomic parable of the novel: the death of her mother on Manhattan's lower East Side as a victim of inhumanity — evidently capitalistically exploitative inhumanity of the sort that Karl's Uncle Jacob finds so exhilarating and praiseworthy. Therese's parabolic narration is intimacy, but not strictly seductive intimacy.

In less retrospective mood, though, Therese is apt to have more seductive—probably innocent-seductive—wiles at her disposal than one might suppose. For example, she often surprises Karl with small presents. One evening while he is on elevator duty, she brings him an apple. This gift apple as the symbol of seduction has not gone completely unnoticed by critics.[8] Nor, by fewer critics, the fact that when Karl finally gains a moment of respite from his arduous but gladly performed duties and can bite into the apple, it gives off a strong aroma just as he has a glimpse into a storeroom where masses of bananas gleam in the darkness. The point here is not so much to develop the Freudian implication of the gleaming bananas after the bite into the fragrant fruit of seduction as to suggest that after even this merely symbolic seduction by Therese, Karl—dutiful, submissive, naive, and guilty (of what?)—is shortly to suffer expulsion and fall.

Karl—who is by no means the last of Kafka's autobiographical "K" heroes—loses his job, he loses the confidence of his friend and protectress, the chief cook. This Viennese woman, incidentally, begins to forsake her advocacy, to cave in—to fall, in a sense—to the pressure of her colleague and Karl's principal denouncer, the headwaiter, shortly after the latter seductively smooths her lace collar; and her abandonment of Karl is all but complete after the headwaiter surreptitiously fondles her hand. Karl is dismissed from the hotel in disgrace, just a hairbreadth from arrest, falling ineluctably into the untender mercies of Delamarche and Robinson, together with their new associate, the corpulent and lascivious Brunelda.

He is held virtually a slave to perform personal services in a household whose physical filth seems calculated to reflect the moral level of the occupants. Brunelda, who has like Karl also fallen out of middle-class life, seems now to be a prostitute under the aegis of the dominant and anarchistic Delamarche, whose mistress she also is, while the subservient Robinson is their voyeuristic servant, who would like to shuffle the more onerous aspects of his role off onto the captive Karl. Nor does Brunelda spare Karl her perhaps dubious seductiveness, as one notes on the occasion of the electoral campaign parade in the coy byplay with which she forces her binocular onto Karl, compelling his head to press against her huge breast. "When on earth are you going to see?"[9] she asks suggestively.

Whether Karl wants to see is most debatable. Besides Brunelda's salacious overture (sandwiched between provocative arrogance and derision and further physical contact) there is Robinson's assurance that being a servant to Brunelda, thus sleeping in the same room with her and Delamarche, offers various advantages not to be found in other jobs. The advantages Robinson refers to have more to do with touching and seeing than with consummation. There is no indication, it is true, that the still-innocent, still-submissive—but in this environment less so—still existentially guilty Karl is attracted by any of them. In the Bruneldian household, however, the inference of seduction is inescapable; and Karl is under, indeed a captive under, the same roof.

The replication of the sequence of seduction and fall, for Brunelda as well as Karl, seems assured if, as revisionist critics now do, one places appendix 2, the fragmentary "Brunelda's Departure," after chapter 7, "A Refuge"—note the ironic chapter title—and before the last chapter, "The Nature Theater of Oklahoma." For Brunelda's departure is a departure from the sexual libertinism of the "Refuge" to a more organized and commercialized form of sex—that is, to a brothel. Karl's still-further fall is characterized by his all too adept performance of his mission in delivering Brunelda to the shabby splendor of Establishment No. 25. Karl already seems to be employed there as a factotum, to judge from the reprimand of the proprietor about his tardiness as well as from Karl's own reticence about his most recent employment when he applies for a post with the Oklahoma Nature Theater.

Even with the inclusion of the two fragmentary chapters after "A Refuge" there is still a wide narrative and structural gap before "The Nature Theater of Oklahoma." To some extent, at least, the discrepancy results from Kafka's having appended a utopian ending to a distinctly nonutopian novel—or perhaps a consistent dream-narrative ending to a quasi-naturalistic, quasi-dream-narrative body—and then having abandoned the novel because the gap is simply too wide to be bridged. It is a fact that he wrote the last chapter two years after having laid aside the first part. It is a further fact that Max Brod gave the last chapter the title, "The Nature Theater of Oklahoma," although there is no internal reference to justify the Nature part. It is by no means certain that the so-called utopian ending is utopian, except in a parodistic sense. In fact as the novel breaks off— the final chapter is also fragmentary—Karl, having resumed a flirtation, or perhaps a closer friendship, is possibly headed toward a final fall: death, or at any rate, disappearance. Or as Kafka was to put it in a diary entry of September 30, 1915: "in the end, punitively killed . . . rather pushed aside than beaten down."[10]

The seduction-fall sequence becomes most problematic in "The Nature Theater of Oklahoma." It might emerge as slightly more persuasive if the reader had available more of the missing parts of the novel between the penultimate and the final chapter. Presumably, that absent portion would acquaint the reader in detail with the nature of Karl's earlier acquaintance with the Fanny whom he meets toward the beginning of the last chapter. Evidently, she is an old friend and a good friend, one with whom he is instantly again on good terms. But the degree of intimacy in the—unnarrated—past can only be conjectured.

Karl meets up with Fanny again when he responds to the recruitment poster of the Oklahoma Theater, which invites prospective members for its company—and it has a place for everyone!—to sign up today, today only, at the Clayton racetrack. There are not many takers, but there is a sign, EVERYONE IS WELCOME, and there is Fanny, a member of the recruiting company, one of hundreds of women dressed as angels, mounted on tall pedestals of varying heights, playing long trumpets vigorously but with a complete absence of harmony. The rapport between Fanny and Karl, however, is more than harmonious: a joyful and (for the reader) agonizingly cryptic reunion of close friends in a fantastic milieu—more consistently fantastic than that of the body of the novel. In the end one does not know whether the fresh start provided by the unconditional—but nicely categorized as to specialty—acceptance for employment in the theater will finally spell happiness for the technical assistant Karl Rossmann or whether his next fall is into oblivion. He never sees Fanny again; they are posted to different troupes of The Oklahoma Theater.

As Karl is on the train headed west with his troupe the novel breaks off with the words: "broad mountain streams appeared, rolling in great waves down on to the foothills and drawing with them a thousand foaming wavelets, plunging underneath the bridges over which the train rushed, and they were so near that the breath of coldness rising from them chilled the skin of one's face."[11] Is that "breath of coldness," one wonders, the breath of the chill of death?

The atmosphere of fantasy in "The Nature Theater of Oklahoma" is reinforced by the fact that it is, precisely, a theater, the very realm of fantasy. Is the reader to understand that Karl's only hope—if it is a hope—lies in fantasy? That, by extension, an innocent—but of course guilty—submissive, enduring, egotistical person's only hope lies in fantasy? That only fantasy is truly endurable? And what if that fantasy is already labeled fantasy, that is, theater—even, as Fanny avers, the biggest theater in the world? Such questions spring to mind, but not the answers.

Everyone is accepted, the theater advertises, and the claim is apparently true. But in small print, so to speak, on the sign that Karl reads—and it's clear that Fanny knows too—is the somewhat ambiguous stipulation, If you want to be an artist, join our company. But presumably the wish suffices, and it is not the habit of the benign company interviewers to test very aggressively the veracity of the applicants' answers. They may steer an interviewee but they do not confute. Indeed, Karl is signed up under the surname Negro because that is the name he gives. And there is no questioning of the wish to be an artist—in this theater even a technical assistant is an artist. But surely Kafka, the highly self-conscious artist mired in a highly unartistic job, is making a broader statement here: it would have to do with the necessity of fantasy in the self-salvation of the artist. This kind of qualification can rarely be avoided when one speaks of Kafka—even if the salvation is itself a fantasy.

Is this fantasy part of a parodistic final chapter? A parody in which the chief themes of the preceding chapters are stood on their heads? Where hostility has prevailed, Karl now finds amicability. Instead of exploitation, acceptance. In place of injustice, suddenly justice. Not only that, but there is on every hand the promise of more and ever-more amicability, acceptance, and justice, under the expansive wing of the Theater of Oklahoma. Is the reader to assume that in the Dickensian manner Karl's probity, his submissiveness, his slightly ridiculous and already slightly parodied desire to oblige—that in the end these shining qualities enable him to win through, to find his reward? This would be in accord with the long-dominant eschatological reading imposed on the novel by Brod, who assembled it and titled it in consonance with his own redemptive philosophy. More recent critics have suggested alternatives. It seems more likely, given that only a fragmentary last chapter is at the reader's disposal, that Kafka the humorist was writing a parodistic spoof of the generic utopian resolution.

Such a parody was particularly appropriate, because in its episodic structure the novel was going nowhere once Karl had been abased and degraded to a point from which it was impossible to sink any lower. (A parodistic reading also amounts to a send-up of Dickens, of whom Kafka was a discerning critic as well as a restrained admirer.) In any case, the ending is jarringly out of synchronization with Karl's earlier life, and Kafka has not narratively linked the two. Presumably because he found it an impossible task.

In the tendency to denominate the final chapter "The Nature Theater of Oklahoma" as radically different from the major portion of the novel, it may be prudent to remind oneself of the links as well as the disparities. As the plight of the hero in *Amerika* is not so different from that in Kafka's works as a whole, or from that in the other novels specifically, so "The Nature Theater of Oklahoma" is not a thing totally apart from the novel to which it is after all linked, although only imperfectly. To reiterate: Karl is the same. His world, if changed drastically, is not without familiar signposts, for example, the allusion to his previous employment or the fact that his professional category remains, in fact is officially designated, as that of a European intermediate school pupil.

Less obviously, a very few key narrative details or motifs from the larger part of the novel are rounded out and completed in the final chapter. For instance, the reappearance of one of Karl's friends from the ranks of the elevator boys at the Hotel Occidental, Giacomo by name, is perhaps not really so incidental as critics customarily imply. For the name Giacomo is simply an Italian version of Jacob. Thus the last chapter is thematically linked not only to the "Hotel Occidental" chapter but through it back to the first three chapters and the problematic Uncle Jacob. Not without thematic irony, of course: if Jacob is the patriarch, as in Genesis, his quondam surrogate son Karl surely wanders, founds no tribe in the new land, and comes full circle in his absorption in Giacomo as the train heads for Oklahoma while the breath of coldness rises from the damp gorges.

Virtually no additional insight into *Amerika* as a whole is afforded by attempting to analyze it as a bildungsroman, a novel in which the hero is formed by his experiences to enter into and prevail in the middle-class world. Karl seemingly learns nothing, or exceedingly little, from his unfortunate experiences in alien America; he remains a European, with the perceptions and expectations — even of a utopia? — of a European. Indeed, all too tellingly, in the final chapter he is still categorized as a European intermediate school pupil. And it is hardly middle-class life that beckons Karl. That is where he is *from* — his parents' home, his Uncle Jacob's home — not where he is going. In fact a major thrust of the novel is his fall, this time in a social sense, down through the proletarian world and into its criminal or semicriminal substrata.

Nor, as has sometimes been suggested, is *Amerika* anything like a picaresque novel. Karl is anything but a streetwise picaro subsisting by playing mean tricks on establishment society. He doesn't act, he is acted upon — and scarcely to his benefit. It may be useful to think of him as being, at least for a time, in a social world common to picaresque novels — the interface of the middle class and the proletarian — and there playing a role quite the reverse of the picaro's.

It has also been suggested that *Amerika* is a naturalistic novel of social reform. Kafka, it is fair to note, from his thoroughly bourgeois vantage point was conspicuously sympathetic — for example, in his field work on insurance cases — with the exploited victims of industrialization in Bohemia. But he was scarcely an Emile Zola or an Upton Sinclair; he might have been that, to judge from his insightful depiction of the results of exploitation, but political and social reform was not the motivating tendency of his art, which has a much wider and at the same time more profoundly metaphysical basis. (And of course he regarded naturalistic writing as the lowest form of writing.)

Kafka was rehabilitated into the Communist canon after decades of ostracism, beginning in the early 1960s and reaching wider public notice through a conference in Prague in 1963. Marxist criticism then and subsequently has occasionally proved illuminating in throwing an unfamiliar light on Kafka, for example that of dynamism. Obviously, Kafka and dynamism make a strange pair — still it is a thought-provoking notion. But for the most part, despite early instances of critical (and apparently even physical) courage vis-à-vis, above all, the Soviet regime, Marxist Kafka criticism is inherently limited by tunnel vision and tired rubrics.

Although *Amerika* has received far less critical attention than *The Trial* or *The Castle* — and Kafka by his own account had not entirely freed himself from naturalistic writing — it is still possible to regard the first novel as more than a merely curious prelude to its successors and as worthy of attention in its own right. As far as its episodic structure is concerned it is not unique; Kafka's novels do not stop being episodic, and they are hardly the less monumental for that. With close reading, *Amerika* may well reveal that it deserves better than the lukewarm critical approbation that is its frequent lot.

4

The Trial

Kafka wrote all but the last chapter of *The Trial* in 1914, within weeks of breaking his first engagement to Felice Bauer. The final chapter dates from 1916. There are also several uncompleted chapters and fragments not included in the body of the novel as published. Kafka gave the manuscript to Brod in 1920. Despite the author's express wish that it be destroyed rather than published, Brod found ample justification for pursuing the latter course after Kafka's death.

It is no difficult task to relate the K-hero of the fiction, in this case Josef K., to the situation of the author at the time he wrote the novel. Kafka had just observed his thirty-first birthday; when the reader meets Josef K. he has just passed his watershed thirtieth birthday. The events of the novel cover one year, and K's assassination occurs on the night before his thirty-first birthday. While there is much, much more than autobiography to be discerned in *The Trial*, it would be critically inadvisable to ignore the obvious relationship to Kafka's life — a relationship that is perhaps the key to most other insights.

It is interesting as well as relevant to note that Kafka enjoyed reading his manuscript of *The Trial* aloud before Brod and other friends and that the first chapter was the source of hearty laughter on the part of the author-reader as well as of the audience. The mirth may be a little hard to credit; but on being appalled or mystified by *The Trial* one ought to keep in mind its jovial first reception—at least of the initial chapter. There is humor in there, and throughout, even some one-liners. Kafka's having read the novel aloud also afforded Brod, years later, some external keys to the sequence of the unnumbered chapters, although internal evidence could suggest a different sequence.

As in *Amerika*, the structure of *The Trial* is episodic. The several characters with whom Josef K. interacts—or, more correctly, fails to interact—tend to disappear and not to return, or to return in something like cameo appearances. In short, they appear and disappear—even sometimes share roles with each other—very much like characters in a dream. Not that K. is dreaming his unhappy—but perhaps also humorous—fate: Kafka's disclaimer, "it was no dream," would be as true for *The Trial* as it was for *The Metamorphosis*. But it is a dream-narrative in the sense that dream logic, or illogic, seems to govern the comings and goings and the interrelationships of the characters, both with K. and with one another, as well as, above all, K.'s relationship with the Court that has him arrested and, after a year of interrogations, hearings, petitions, and inaccessibility, executed. At the same time, K.'s plight is not that of needing to break through from dream to reality; the reader does well not to be as concerned as K. is about the nature of the Law that hounds him, but rather to focus on K. himself and his evidently flawed responses to the Law.

With these chilling lines—only from the political point of view are they more suitable to the mid- and late-twentieth century than to the era in which Kafka wrote—*The Trial* commences: "Someone must have traduced Josef K., for without having done anything wrong he was arrested one fine morning."[1] But it would be extremely limiting to restrict ourselves to a merely political exegesis of *The Trial*, to take K. as a man caught up in the inexplicable and labyrinthine bureaucracy of the doddering Hapsburg Empire. As far as that approach goes, while the pre-World War I Austrian bureaucracy — of which Kafka as a legally trained semigovernmental insurance representative was himself a member — was indeed pervasive and sometimes callous, it was not on the whole evil or monstrously inhumane in the sense that the subsequent Nazi bureaucracy was. Josef K.'s arrest — but then not quite arrest either, as it turns out — is a mystery beyond any political denominator.

The two warders who first invade his bedroom — with K. still in bed — and arrest him fail to oblige his demand to know what he is charged with. The lowest order of Court officialdom — ignorant oafs in the view of K., a high-ranking bank officer very conscious of his own social superiority — the warders do not know the charge. K., however, is given to understand that his arrest has been preceded by a thorough investigation; the Law is not given to frivolous accusation. Indeed the Law's officials are said not to go hunting for crime; rather they are drawn toward the guilty and then dispatch the warders to make the arrests. At K.'s objection that he knows nothing of such a Law, he is informed, significantly one may eventually conclude, that it probably exists only in his own head.

As a banker, K. is not entirely ignorant of law. In what Kafka may well have intended, and then deleted, as an opening chapter of *The Trial*,[2] K. is introduced as a confidant, first, of the bank's attorney, and then, above all, of one Hasterer, the district attorney, and as a member of a lunch table comprised almost entirely of lawyers and judges, from whose professional chatter and hypothetical cases he learns much. In any case, in the first chapter as published K. is so thrown off his guard, so deprived of the protection provided by the bank's hierarchy and his own considerable power there that he fails to use his wits very effectively. He cuts a rather silly appearance, for example, in rummaging through a drawer after his bicycle license, with the presentation of which he hopes to get the warders off his case. Humorous this is too, especially if the reader has not already begun contemplating the ominousness of the other details of K.'s apprehension: the abruptness, the intransigence of the warders, the absence of a specific charge, and simply the ambiguous nature of the arrest itself.

For K. is not hauled off to jail. The warders, having greedily consumed K.'s own breakfast, even offer to fetch him a take-out breakfast from the coffeehouse across the street. But K., haughtily disdaining the product of what he regards as a greasy spoon, instead bites into an apple he has saved from the previous evening. If the apple plays the same biblically tainted role as it does for Karl Rossmann in *Amerika* and in different fashion for Gregor Samsa in *The Metamorphosis*, the attentive reader may guess that nothing good is in the offing for K. Apparently sensing the same, K. fortifies himself with two glasses of brandy.

The inspector, however, who arrives to give K. a preliminary hearing on the scene, although standing on his prerogatives, is not unconciliatory. He, like the warders, can give K. no particulars of the charge—just the reiteration of the cold fact that K. is under arrest. Still, he can offer a piece of highly important advice. "Think less about us and of what is going to happen to you," he recommends, "think more about yourself instead" (17). Especially is this true, one may be tempted to add in response to the repeated advertence to the fact that this is K.'s thirtieth birthday, especially now that you, K., have crossed the final bridge into adulthood and ought to be capable of mature introspection rather than seizing on every pretext to rationalize and argue. For K.'s precocious success in the banking business—at age thirty he is second or third in importance at his bank—stands in pronounced contrast to his immaturity in the personal realm. For example, his emotional life consists in having loveless sex once a week with a promiscuous cabaret waitress named Elsa.

To conduct K.'s on-site hearing, the inspector sets up a hearing room in the downstairs room of another of Frau Grubach's tenants, a Fräulein Bürstner, who is absent all day at her job as a typist—next month she will be joining the clerical staff of a lawyer's office. While Kafka never discloses Fräulein Bürstner's first name, the attentive reader notes that the initials F. B. coincide with those of Felice Bauer, with whom Kafka had just recently broken. In his manuscript he regularly refers to Fräulein Bürstner by the initials F. B.

Spectators at K.'s hearing include a salacious old couple in the window across the way—one thinks of Mr. and Mrs. Samsa's coital embrace before the horrified Gregor in *The Metamorphosis*—and in the hearing room itself the two warders as well as three unidentified anemic young men who seem to have wandered in from nowhere, standing around idly, regarding K. gravely, and evincing an impertinent interest in Fräulein Bürstner's personal photographs. The inspector presses Fräulein Bürstner's nightstand into service as a kind of central desk.

In addition to the evasions, reprimands, and advice on the part of the inspector, he confirms that while K. is indeed under arrest, he is not to be hindered from going about his business, from leading what the inspector—surely humorously—terms "your ordinary life." He has detained the three hitherto unidentified young men for the purpose of accompanying K. to his workplace—the three are in fact subordinates of K. at the bank, as he now suddenly perceives. That he has failed to identify them previously lends substance to the incommensurability of his two worlds, the professional and the personal. So automated are his responses and so wide is the chasm between these two worlds, that he is unable to effect the most obvious identifications without the aid of context. True, everyone has known the sensation of forgetting a familiar person's name on seeing that person away from familiar surroundings. But K., confronted with three such persons, and in a group, can only be judged particularly obtuse on that score. His perceptions are rigid and compartmented. This seems especially significant in the light of his celebrating his thirtieth birthday, a landmark in life at which such a disadvantage is apt to be fixed, not susceptible to a more flexible awareness of oneself and one's world. An awareness of which, it becomes repeatedly evident, Josef K. stands in sore need.

On the evening of this, his thirtieth birthday, duly marked by the friendly and flattering birthday wishes of his colleagues at the bank, K. returns straight home. He feels the need to apologize to his landlady, Frau Grubach, for the disturbance resulting from his arrest that morning. For all his civility toward her, K. regards her as stupid, and that is the denominator by which he responds with ostensible civility but probably genuine irony to her insight: "What you've just said is by no means stupid, Frau Grubach." (26). What she has just said, very deferentially, admitting the possibility of its being stupid, is that K.'s arrest gives her "the feeling of something learnéd which I don't understand, but which there is no need to understand." Were his mind and attitude of a less-rigid, less-self-justifying cast, K. would have understood and adopted Frau Grubach's profoundly simple advice to quit trying intellectually to understand the Law that ordered his arrest — and, inferentially, to begin trying to understand himself, to get in touch with himself. But he cannot manage it. The rest of the novel depends on his persistent adherence — is that persistence in itself somehow laudable? — to his false tack.

That there is at least some validity to what Frau Grubach is saying, he does recognize; but his recognition takes on only the dull coloration of rationalization and guilt. Who is really stupid here? Kafka seems to imply humorously. The guilt is vague and undifferentiated, by later critics called existential. It, as well as his false direction, reveals itself early on. For example: Frau Grubach observes that she has twice met up with Fräulein Bürstner in the company of men and she, Frau Grubach, is extremely concerned about keeping her house respectable. "'Respectable!' cried K., 'if you want to keep your house respectable you'll have to begin by giving me notice'" (29).

K. too is attracted to Fräulein Bürstner, if ambiguously. While on the one hand he feels no special desire to see her, on the other hand he does want to talk to her. He is annoyed, first, that her proximity and influence have caused him to postpone one of his weekly visits to Elsa and, second, that it is after 11 P.M. and she hasn't come home yet. When she arrives and he tries to explain the arrest hearing held in her room that morning, she proves an amused and witty respondent, highly respectable but certainly sexually attractive as well. K. botches things badly, forcing a greedy kiss on his unwilling respondent "like some thirsty animal." Yet on reflection he is pleased with his behavior—which doubtless says something about his inability to bring any real sensitivity to his relationship with others or even to his own self-perception.

On receiving the summons to his first interrogation—not counting the arrest hearing in Fräulein Bürstner's room—K. is resolved to fight. He will accede to the summons but he is resolved that the first interrogation shall also be the last. Not the least factor in his determination to show up at the unlikely address—in a tenement district—is his desire to learn the nature of his adversary and the case against him. Of what, again, precisely is he charged, and what is the Law or the Court that accuses him? Again one may infer that K.'s focus here is misdirected. Instead of fighting, it would be better if he yielded. Rather than knowledge of his opponent, it would be better if he were to gain knowledge of himself. He is doing it all wrong.

The Court is not easy to find, in an attic room of a tenement occupied—on a Sunday—by whole families of workers as well as their laundry. But at this early stage of his case K. is strong and determined and resistant. The Court session is more like a political meeting—in fact in Kafka's earlier version it was a Socialist meeting—crowds of poorly clad people on both sides of the aisle, a cramped balcony in which the spectators cannot stand upright without hitting their heads on the ceiling. Everywhere a sense of crowdedness. And everywhere a corresponding, indeed exaggerated oppressiveness in the air: too many people, too little air, too much sun beating down on the roof, too much dirt. The fetidness will take its toll on K.

But for the time—he is late, although no appointed hour had been given him—K. makes fine speeches in his defense, with pointed reference to the unfairness, the impropriety of it all. Probably Kafka's earlier description of the assemblage as a Socialist meeting he later judged to be too bald, too unsuggestive a contrast to K.'s own social level. But a court session, prosecution and defense, makes the point in a more dynamic way. (Marxist criticism often imposes dynamic readings on Kafka; in this instance it could be appropriate.) K. is a self-made, middle-class striver, a great success as a businessman but, as the reader has begun to perceive, a sad failure as a human being. He exhibits, especially against the background of the tenement Court of Inquiry and its officials, too many of the infelicitous qualities of his kind: defensiveness, snobbishness, arrogance, a lack of openness, and a tendency to think of women, particularly working-class women, as objects.

K. proceeds to humiliate the examining magistrate before the assemblage, which only slightly later, on his noting the badges on their collars under their clawlike beards, is revealed to him as being comprised wholly of officials of the Court. He reiterates his denunciation of the lowly warders who first placed him under arrest as well as the way in which the arrest was made. He berates the organization behind his arrest, what he perceives as its corruption, and the senseless-ness of the proceedings against him. The tirade by which K. dominates the session is interrupted only by a shriek and a disturbance from the back of the hall. Although the dim light and the haze in the reeking room make identification difficult, it appears to be the young dark-eyed woman who had directed him to the meeting room, now in the sexual embrace of a man near the rear door (the outcry was his), much to the delight of the assembled officials, who may well have been getting tired of K.'s spellbinding.

When K. in high dudgeon makes to leave, the examin-ing magistrate reproaches him: "Today you have flung away with your own hand all the advantages which an interroga-tion inevitably confers on an accused man" (60). The reader no doubt should accept ironically the notion that the magis-trate is concerned to provide help to K., help that in any case K. spurns with his pompous self-righteousness and headlong departure. Indications are accumulating that K., with whom the reader inclines to identify, because he is the persecuted and because he is at least more sympathetic than his collec-tive adversary, is going about things completely wrong. His task — to put it in slightly different terms than heretofore — is not to track down the essence of his adversary and its case against him, but rather to look within himself. Not, almost surely, that that will save him either. In the process — the German title of the novel, *Der Prozess*, means first, "the trial," and secondarily, "the process" — his plight has its hu-morous as well as its ominous overtones. The same may be said of his consistent overreactions. Of course, he is desper-ate and will increasingly have cause to be so — but, in a sense, he is never quite desperate enough.

Receiving no summons for the next Sunday, K. nevertheless returns to the strangely situated Court that has juris-
diction over his case. His goal, his blindly and thus incorrectly formed goal, is "to assure himself that the inside of this
legal system was just as loathsome as its external aspect" (83).
It evidently is; but that is hardly germane to his guilt that he
is unable to confront — or, no, perhaps the system does just
begin to instill an inchoate impression of guilt, but not one
that is focused or useful.

Retracing his steps on the second Sunday, K. is greeted
by the dark-eyed woman involved in the sexual encounter
that ended his speechmaking a week ago. The meeting
room, except on meeting days, is the apartment she shares
with her husband. The public sexual embrace, she explains,
was with a student, a rising young star of the Court, and
"there's no way of keeping him off" (63). K. himself makes
advances to her; he wants to inspect the magistrate's law
books that are in her care. "How dirty everything is here!" he
exclaims before opening the first book, which proves to contain a dirty picture. The dark-eyed woman, the usher's wife,
it emerges, is sexually available not only to the precocious
student Bertold but by way of him to the chief magistrate as
well. As Bertold carries her off, he snaps with his teeth at the
hand of K., with whom she purportedly had been willing to
flee.

K. pauses to take superficial stock of his situation. The
defection of the dark-eyed woman is the first unequivocal
defeat he has suffered at the hands of the Court's people.
His superiority to them would have been better maintained,
he now sees, if he had stayed at home, away from contact
with them. He fantasizes the sexually aggressive student
pleading in vain for Elsa's favors. It may be useful here for
the reader to compare on the one hand the middle-class K.'s
orderly, regularized, aseptic satisfaction of his sexual needs
with, on the other hand, the rather violent, irregular, sponta-

neous sexual responses of the proletarians associated with the court. K. makes no such explicit comparison; he limits himself rather to comparing his orderly, tidy professional existence in a spacious office behind a plate-glass window with that of the chief magistrate in a dirty garret.

The frequent authorial attention to the social chasm does not, however, as Marxist-oriented critics imagine, mean that Kafka is engaged in a novel of social protest — let alone in writing Socialist realism. Rather, the social gulf, by feeding K.'s self-satisfaction, by propping up his self-righteous ego in its travail from outer insult and assault, serves to divert him from, blind him to, the imperative of turning inward, of declaring not his legal innocence but his existential guilt.

In the course of K.'s tour of the upstairs offices of the Court under the guidance of the usher, he observes to himself that the numerous accused waiting in the lobby "obviously belonged to the upper classes" (78). His further indulgence in social stereotyping amounts to further fundamental obfuscation. On courteously asking a gray-haired accused man, "What are you waiting for?" K. receives a vague nonresponse that at once recalls K.'s own past puzzlement at his arrest and foretells his confusion. A moment later he finds himself tired and faint, oppressed by the foul air, wanting only to be assisted to an exit. Unable to find the way out by himself, he wants only to be accompanied — not merely directed — there. He is so sick he has to sit down, he can no longer walk without being assisted on either side. In his passivity he hears a voice declaring, "You can tell him a hundred times that the door is in front of him and he makes no move to go" (90). The reader who wishes a succinct thematic statement may keep in mind the above indication of K.'s nonmovement; it, or something very much like it, will recur in a summary parable some few chapters later.

In the following short chapter, chapter 4, K. tries in vain

to exchange a brief word with Fräulein Bürstner, a word supposedly of apology for his clumsy and less than welcome advances the other night, for having possibly damaged her reputation in the eyes of the other lodgers by being in her room at night. His intent is unrealized, however; instead he is forced to listen at length to Fräulein Bürstner's talkative representative and new roommate, Fräulein Montag. Not surprisingly, perhaps, he takes solace in the smug reflection that Fräulein Bürstner was after all an ordinary little typist not likely to resist him for long.

K.'s actions in the trenchant and dreamlike chapter, "The Whipper," are even less calculated to make the reader suppose that K. is gaining any insight as to why it is that he has been accused. Of course, ever since he finally recognized the three bank underlings at the scene of his arrest—not to speak of having encountered them on the street when he was going to his first interrogation—he has been worried about the threat that his case poses to his rather exalted status at the bank. Very consciously as well as subconsciously—as the reader has observed—his actions are calculated to keep these two worlds apart.

But how can this be managed when, on hearing convulsive sighs behind the door of a storage room at the bank, he enters to find a whipper clad in dark leather beating two men whom K. belatedly recognizes as his former warders? They are being whipped, so they shout, because K. complained about them to the chief magistrate. Honestly enough K. replies that he did not demand that they be punished. In what the reader may regard as an oblique reference to K.'s own case, the whipper retorts that despite excuses the punishment he is meting out to the two warders is inevitable.

K., moved perhaps more by the threat to him of the whipping occurring on bank premises than by the cruel and unjust punishment inflicted on the bumbling warders, attempts, without success, to bribe the whipper to cease. Quickly slamming the door as he leaves the storage room, he assures the two advancing bank clerks that the noise is only a dog howling in the courtyard and orders them to return to their work. Reflecting, he feels disappointed at his inability to prevent the whipping, but then it was not his fault that he had not succeeded. And at a certain point the shrieks of one of the warders has made intervention impossible. At least, one might add, intervention on the part of Josef K. The next day, when he opens the door to the storage room, everything is still the same. He orders the clerks to clear out the storage room; "we're being smothered in dirt!" (111). That dirt is surely not limited—even within the confines of the storage room—to such physical things as the bundles of old paper, and the discarded ink bottles.

As much as to defend his legal innocence, K.'s battle is to enforce mutual exclusivity on his two worlds, that of his case and that of his profession. If in the first battle signs of defeat are gathering—paradoxically seeming to reinforce his staunch insouciance—the second as well seems an increasingly dubious battle. He tries to keep up a front at the bank but, possibly passed by the three witnesses to his arrest, the word is out. K.'s Uncle Karl is informed and hastens to the city from his country retreat to offer help to his nephew. K., however, is not especially keen to accept help from this "ghost from the past," that is, K.'s childhood—evidently another walled-off world in K.'s cosmos.

K.'s inability to grasp the extent of the seriousness of his situation, to treat his adversaries with the earnestness they merit, is a pervasive theme, reiterated tellingly in the chapter entitled "K.'s Uncle—Leni." K. may have a glimmer of perception in declining his uncle's suggestion that he go to the countryside as a way of reducing the pressure to which he is subject. No, says K., that would look like flight and therefore guilt. One is struck first by the fact that in this case

K.'s sagacity matches his passivity—by doing nothing he has the opportunity of imagining that he is exercising good judgment. Second, one is struck by the humorous paradox: after all, K. *is* guilty already; going to the country would scarcely affect his guilt.

K. is almost as reluctant to accompany his uncle to a consultation with the lawyer Huld, his uncle's classmate. Huld turns out to be ill but nonetheless already well-informed, through the professional grapevine, about K.'s case. Indeed, also visiting Huld at the moment is the chief clerk of the Court, whose face K. fancies he remembers from among the audience—the first row of the audience—at his first interrogation. But while Uncle Karl, Huld, and the chief clerk confer, where is K.? Seducing, or perhaps being seduced by, the ardent Leni, lawyer Huld's nurse and—as Uncle Karl witheringly informs K. later—"obviously the lawyer's mistress." Not an unhumorous situation—but not an auspicious one for K.'s defense either.

In addition to her considerable sex drive (she exults in displacing Elsa), Leni is endowed with no small psychic insight. At least, having heard that K. is too unyielding, she believes it to be true and advises, "You must confess to guilt" (135). Leni also has what she calls a slight physical defect: on her right hand there is a connecting web of skin between two of her fingers. K. affectionately holds her slightly deformed hand, but despite his almost-willful damage to his own legal case—making love with Leni—he is a long way from being persuaded to the confession of guilt that might, or might not, make his case moot. Certainly innocence does not guarantee definite acquittal, as the Court painter Titorelli will make amply clear to him.

K. becomes persuaded that Titorelli, an effective advocate—frank and apparently ingenuous—is more promising than the sick and self-justifying lawyer Huld. Ironically enough, the lawyer's name means "grace" or "favor" in German. But even before K. finds his way to Titorelli's squalid tenement—in fact, just about the time that the thought of his case comes to dominate his mind—K. convinces himself that Huld is completely ineffective and resolves to dismiss him, even though such a step by an accused is unheard of. No longer holding his own case in contempt, K. feels Titorelli's personal intervention to be absolutely essential. In his hubris, perhaps also as a reflex of his lawyerly associations— even Titorelli will tell him, "You are almost as good as a lawyer yourself" (171)—K. imagines that in key respects his case is like a business deal and determines to draw up his own plea.

Little does he realize that this step, like every other he has taken, will only draw him more tightly into the toils of the Court, will only crumble further the already eroding barriers between his all-important career—read careerism— and his increasingly threatening case. For it will require much time to draw up his plea, and that necessity is in conflict with the demands of his work. A leave of absence is possible, but that would be certain to put his career rival, the assistant manager, in possession of knowledge about K.'s case. In his preoccupation and growing exhaustion, K. is already emerging as in no shape to conduct complicated business negotiations with the bank's clients. (The assistant manager is all too happy to supplant him and to ransack K.'s files.)

It is just one such cheated client, however, who reveals to K. that he has been told of K.'s case by a man called Titorelli. That client offers the opinion that the artist, who worked for the Court, might indeed be useful to K. K.'s waning powers of judgment are shown in his unthinking decision to write Titorelli. Write—with a case hanging over his head? The bank client disabuses him of the wisdom of such a self-incriminating step, but K. now begins to realize, as the attentive reader has for some little while realized, that

on a path fraught with peril K. unalertly exposes himself to
even more peril by his tendency to follow every false path.
As his alertness and vitality decrease, his risk grows.

Besides K.'s own obtuse reactions, principal stations of
his downward course are signaled—effectively foretold—by
episodes of more or less lewd sexuality, somewhat as the
stations of Karl Rossmann's downward course in *Amerika* are
preceded by episodes of seduction or the suggestion of seduction. In the case of K., the reader remembers, in addition
to his weekly sex dates with Elsa the cabaret waitress, his
violently greedy kissing of Fräulein Bürstner, his relationship to the promiscuous dark-eyed wife of the usher at the
Court office, complete with the uncovering of a lewd picture in the law book, and his intercourse with Leni, Huld's
nurse and mistress. Now, outside the painter Titorelli's studio, he comes into contact with a band of girls of about
thirteen years of age, at once teasingly childish and de-
praved—especially a hunchback whose eyes already reveal
her availability. K., however, is apparently uninterested in
girls that young and brushes by them—but before he leaves
Titorelli's, he will have an unwelcome surprise that constitutes another ominous station on his downward course.

At the outset, the painter sympathetically acquaints
him with further details of Court procedure, with the nature
of its justice, and with the three kinds of acquittal possible,
thereupon volunteering to represent K.'s interests before the
Court. But the reader may well reflect that none of this is
really in K.'s interest. His real business is not to obtain information about his institutional adversary, but about himself.

One of the first sensations K. feels in Titorelli's
cramped living quarters and studio is the stifling air. Although K. doesn't verbalize the connection, the reader's first
thought is of the similarly oppressive air at the tenement
Court and offices across town. Titorelli's credentials as a
painter seem valid, and in this respect K. notices the striking

resemblance between a portrait in the studio and a portrait he had remarked at Huld's prior to his amorous preliminaries with Leni. The latter portrait, so to speak, is of a judge rampant, springing vigorously from a high thronelike seat as if perhaps pronouncing an emphatic judgment. (It is actually a much-glorified picture of an examining magistrate, who posed sitting on a kitchen chair.) Titorelli's judge, on the other hand, is, according to the artist, a representation of Justice and the goddess of Victory, as one. At a certain moment the whole strikes K. as looking like the goddess of the Hunt in full cry.

Titorelli's relation to the Court, as Court painter, is unofficial, thus possibly influential. He proposes a more active defensive posture than Huld seems to favor. It is necessary, according to Titorelli, to distinguish between what is written in the Law and what he has discovered through personal experience behind the scenes, where, with good fortune, acquaintanceship and influence can be brought to bear to prevent a case from actually coming up in a formal way before the higher Court. For once a case is formally brought before it, a higher Court can never be dislodged from its a priori persuasion of guilt. No single person could influence such a Court to a decree of definite acquittal.

The judges of lower rank are empowered only to decree ostensible acquittal in response to a concentrated effort by the defendant and his counsel, or indefinite postponement, requiring continual but less-intense defensive effort. In the case of ostensible acquittal, the charges may be reinstituted at any time. One may sympathize with K. in his need for time to consider which sort of acquittal he ought to aim for, as well as in his hurried assent—he is suffocating in the stale air—to buying some of Titorelli's paintings: heathscapes all exactly identical to one another.

To avoid the gang of childish harlots still hanging around outside Titorelli's, K. leaves via a small passageway whose entrance necessitates his walking over Titorelli's bed. He will stay in touch with Titorelli. Or will he? One may share his discomfiture at discovering that the even more stifling passageway gives on Court offices such as he had experienced in the crosstown tenement. Titorelli is astounded at his ignorance: "There are Law Court offices in almost every attic. . . ." K. is now susceptible to shock at his own ignorance of all things concerning the Court. Despite, it may be added, his by now almost obsessive striving to gain knowledge about it. In a sense then, the harder he strives the more ignorant he feels — more, it is correct to say, than when he was completely ignorant. But his relative knowledge or ignorance of the workings of the Court apparently is not leading him much closer to an acquittal. Indeed, Titorelli with his extensive behind-the-scenes knowledge of the Court, has never known a single instance of definite acquittal. The innocence professed by K. and the guilt presumed by the Court are incommensurable, and in his redoubled ignorance K. cannot mitigate the latter. Having just been factually enlightened by Titorelli in a way that he feels to be much superior to the obscure enlightenment of Huld (Huld's apartment is always dark, shadowy, barely illuminated), K. finds agencies of the Court almost literally popping up all around him. Even the band of girls pursuing him, Titorelli explains, is the property of the Court. Because the Court owns everything.

Kafka never completed the next chapter, the eighth in the novel as published by Brod, dwelling on K.'s extended visit to Huld with the intention of dismissing him from the case. As if to balance the lacuna at the end of the chapter there is a sense of repetitiveness at the start, where the reader is informed that "at long last K. had made up his mind to take his case out of the lawyer's hands" (207). Has he not already come to that conclusion in the middle of the preceding chapter? No matter — except perhaps that the reader is reminded in yet another way that the novel was not in a form that Kafka regarded as publishable when he laid it aside. It may be that Kafka's novel structure, here and elsewhere, *is* basically episodic; but it behooves the thoughtful reader to grant the possibility that the episodes might have been stitched together more smoothly in a final version by the author.

The author does not simply march his bedeviled hero up to lawyer Huld to say "you're fired!" Rather K. is intercepted by another visitor at the lawyer's apartment, who serves as a contrast figure to K. Or, more precisely, as an illustration of what K. will be like when his case has dragged on for five and a half years rather than the mere six months that it has been going on so far—perhaps especially if he does not dismiss the lawyer. This pathetic illustration of K.'s possible future is provided by one Block, a grain trader, although his formerly expansive enterprise has by now dwindled to a two-man operation—or even less, since Block spends days on end at the lawyer's, even sleeping there.

K. is initially mystified by Block's status in the household, taking him for a servant, then for Leni's lover. He puts Block to a little test, asking him to identify the portrait of the examining magistrate, the judge rampant. "It is a high judge," Block offers, whereas the right answer would have been "the lowest of the low." Thus have the rigors of his five-and-a-half-year-long case affected Block's memory and insight—a powerful lesson for K., who within recent weeks has felt his own mental and physical powers waning alarmingly.

It is Leni who identifies Block as another client of Huld's. She is of course delighted to see K., who, without actually dismissing the lawyer, has nonetheless been absenting himself. "But you're certainly going to spend the night with me" (212), she suggests cheerfully, not even curious about the identification of K.'s "momentous" surprise for the lawyer. But while K. waits for the still-ailing lawyer to finish his soup, Block engages his attention and, increasingly, his self-concerned interest. Before the onset of acute self-concern, K. is reassured by the news that Huld conducts an ordinary practice as well as taking cases like Block's and K.'s—reassured, because that indicates at least some kind of connection between the Court and orthodox jurisprudence. The bad news is: Block's case has consumed not only Block's time but his money and energies as well. Trying, for a while, to conduct his own case was unwise; it is impossible to keep up with "things beyond reason"; one becomes "tired and distracted." The case does not move. People become aware of one's plight, inevitably, as the case dawdles. Huld is only a small lawyer, but the way to the great lawyers is unknown. And even with Huld one can wait up to three days for a consultation, one has to be ready night and day—thus Block's makeshift living quarters in what had been the maid's cubicle. This is a cheerless litany for K., who comes to understand that dismissing Huld will not solve many problems either. Quite literally, K. is damned if he does and damned if he does not.

Huld begins the consultation by informing K. that his nurse Leni finds all accused men attractive—accused men are attractive simply by virtue of their being accused. Huld accepts K.'s dismissal coolly, almost as if it were not really definitive. All clients reach this stage. He proceeds to humiliate Block, converting him into a pitiable, fawning animal, a dog—demonstrating to K. what sort of treatment is accorded to accused men whom he, Huld, indulges less than he has indulged K. Despite K.'s distaste for his uncle and his evocation of the past, when K. was a child, it strikes the reader that the avuncular connection may have saved K. from Block's awful fate: to be tormented by rumor, teased by innuendo, reproached for pessimism, despised for fear. And here the uncompleted chapter breaks off, followed some-

what abruptly by the penultimate chapter, "In the Cathedral," which is comprised of two sections.

In the first section, K. is narratively maneuvered into
the cathedral. In the second, he is there told a parable that
applies strikingly to his own predicament. From the beginning K. is reluctant to serve as guide to the visiting Italian
client, or perhaps correspondent, of the bank. He sees such
an assignment, however justified by his modest command of
Italian and his equally modest knowledge of the art works in
the cathedral, as a diversion of his already-diminished energies — so essential to retain his prestige at the bank, to avoid
the increasing number of mistakes that he commits, and to
fend off the insidious rivalry of the assistant manager. K. is
besieged by fear (the word recurs with emphatic frequency).
Moreover he has a severe cold and a racking headache (surely deriving from stress as much as exposure), and the weather for the Italian's visit is miserable — cold, rainy, dark. The
visitor himself turns out to be a humorous pastiche of the
stock Italian as viewed by a central or northern European.
Impeccably dressed, he is not only garrulous but waves his
hands while he speaks. He observes the forms of sociability
and courtesy; but he is apparently unable to speak slowly
with any consistency and seems hardly to care, in any case,
whether he is understood. He continually strokes his
bushy — and apparently perfumed — mustache (the reader is
reminded of the Court people playing with their beards). To
top off the almost stock-humorous situation, K. can understand only fragmentarily the Italian's southern dialect, while
K.'s manager, who performs the introductions, understands
it well, so that K. is constantly trying to tune out the Italian's
ceaseless flow of words while at the same time endeavoring
to pick up the manager's concise German summaries.

Both humorous and ominous are K.'s preliminary bat-
tles with his Italian grammar book the night before. In spite

of working half the night at it, his elaborate copying and sounding out and memorizing of words apt to be useful in an art tour of the cathedral all come to naught, because his formerly excellent memory seems to have deserted him. His case before the Court is taking its toll.

The Italian fails to meet K. at the cathedral as agreed — which, in view of the awful weather, is as sensible as it is discourteous (thus in his case doubly unexpected). But K. feels obliged to wait in the cathedral in case the visitor shows up late. In any event the pouring rain does not suggest a prompt departure, although K. feels an almost frantic urge to get back to his office and catch up on his work.

After examining the finely wrought great pulpit, previously unknown to him — it is clear that K. visits churches more for the art than the religion — by pure chance he espies a verger gesturing to him, pointing, signaling to be followed. K. complies. The verger, his role evidently fulfilled, leaves K. in the vicinity of a small side pulpit, simple and austere, in marked contrast to the great pulpit. Not only is it simple, but the vaulting of its stone canopy begins so far down and curves upward in such a way that a man of average height would not be able to stand upright beneath it. If K. is perhaps too preoccupied to verbalize the comparison, the alert reader will have already recalled the peculiar balcony in the tenement meeting hall where K. first made speeches to the Court, a balcony so close to the ceiling that the spectators put cushions on their heads to dampen the harder bumps.

Above the side pulpit the lamp is on; a priest ascends the stairs. To give a sermon, K. wonders, to a congregation of one or two? — for the cathedral is almost entirely deserted. K. prepares to leave, only to be brought up short by the priest's single sharp cry, "Josef K.!" On K.'s confirming his identity — what a relief, for once, not to be known on sight in his role of accused! — the priest replies, "Then you are the man I seek. . . . I had you summoned here" (263). He is the prison chaplain, thus an official of the Court, and he relays the news that K.'s case is going badly. K. asserts his innocence, together with his interlocutor providing a concise interential definition of existential guilt. "'But I am not guilty,' said K.; 'it's a mistake. And, if it comes to that, how can any man be called guilty? We are all simply men here, one as much as the other.' 'That is true,' said the priest, 'but that's how all guilty men talk'" (264).

The priest charges K. with having too much outside help in his case. (When, the reader wonders, does not enough become too much?) And especially from women — a charge clearly aimed at K.'s tireless pursuit of women in the undifferentiated role of helpers/sex objects. Implicit is the point that K. ought to be more his own man. "Can't you see one pace before you?" shrieks the priest.

A conciliatory conversation follows — which, however, evidences all too clearly K.'s reliance or dependence on others, even on the priest, whom K. regards as "an exception among those who belong to the Court" (267). This is a delusion, replies the priest, you are entertaining a delusion about the Court. And to adumbrate the delusion he tells the parable of the man from the country and the doorkeeper. This, perhaps by virtue of its conceivably explicatory function in the novel — but Kafka's parables typically do not so much explain as offer a metaphor of truth — is surely the most celebrated of Kafka's many parables.

As the priest tells it, a doorkeeper is standing guard before the Law. A man from the country approaches and begs for admittance to the Law. The doorkeeper refuses, even as he seems to hint that his refusal is not necessarily definitive. The man from the country, persistent yet intimidated, sits and waits. The days become years, and he becomes an old man. Perhaps near death, he asks the doorkeeper why — since everyone strives to attain the Law — no one else has sought admittance. The doorkeeper, preparing to close the door, replies that the door was intended only for him.

Critics have suggested a welter of interpretations, not necessarily mutually exclusive. Kafka as narrator, in the mouths of K. and the priest, offers the perhaps basic possibilities in the succeeding text of the novel. But at a certain level of interpretational ramification the reader may be inclined to entertain the possibility that Kafka, a lawyer by training and profession, has moved into legalistic parody. In any case K. promptly takes the view that the doorkeeper deceived the man from the country, that the priest's first interpretation — or really prediction — was quite right: the purpose of the parable is to inveigh against delusion. What neither K. nor the priest admits, however, is that such an interpretation would require the establishment of an equation between delusion on the one hand, inwardly caused, and deception on the other hand, externally imposed. Accusing K. of altering the story in his assignment of blame to the doorkeeper for deferring the essential information, the priest asserts that there is *no* contradiction between the doorkeeper's initial prohibition and his terminal information, and thus no deception.

Maybe, the priest continues, the doorkeeper, a simple soul, was the deluded party. K. can concede this point in the context of *both* parties being deluded. But the priest objects that the doorkeeper, as a representative of the Law, is in any case exempt from being judged. "It is not necessary," he concludes, "to accept everything as true, one must only accept it as necessary" (276). The relevance of such a dictum to K.'s plight is obvious — as well as the priest's earlier reference to the man's cursing loudly "the fate for which he himself is responsible" (272).[3] But K., tired as he is from the convoluted argumentation — and suffering in addition from the fatigue of his case and his work — objects finally that the dictum of necessity over truth "turns lying into a universal principle"

(276). The reader, helped along by this dreary conclusion, may be quite as tired as K. is of analyzing the parable. Kafka almost implies as much from a conceivably tongue-in-cheek stance.

The desire of the fatigued K. to leave the cathedral and resume his role as chief clerk of a bank contends with a paradoxical desire to talk yet further with the priest—who, however, withdraws his apparent friendliness. K.'s expression of his need for guidance in finding his way out of the cathedral cannot help but recall to the attentive reader his similar pleas when he felt it imperative to get out of the Court's offices and into the open air. Not that the air in the cathedral is stifling. Kafka does not overdo simplism. The reader has noted only the oppressively low-hanging vaulting over the side pulpit.

Of more thematic importance is the fact that in the chapter "In the Cathedral" the line that separates K.'s bank and the Court, his two fundamental—and fundamentally opposed—worlds, is dissolving. The reader, focusing consistently on K.'s unfulfilled and seemingly unfulfillable exculpation, should resist the natural temptation to try to solve the problem of the disappearing—or even appearing—Italian as though it were a case for detectives. It can't be done. Rather, one can profitably regard the Italian as the avenue, as the agency that dissolves the protective line K. has drawn between bank and Court.

The Italian is introduced as a friend of the business, the bank. The plan at first is for him to see several tourist attractions in—presumably—Prague. Possibly influenced by the miserable weather, he then proposes to limit his touristic viewing and K.'s guiding to the cathedral only. The manager originally intended to escort the Italian. Then, perhaps owing to his chronic ill health—K. notes that he looks especially unwell this morning—or to his poor state of health plus the weather, the manager decides that K. had better under-

take the role of escort and guide. With the failure of the
Italian to show up, K. is thus fatefully, it would seem, thrust
into the one-on-one meeting with the priest, the prison
chaplain who belongs to the Court. Before leaving his office
at half past nine to meet the Italian at the cathedral at ten
o'clock, K. receives a telephone call from Leni wishing him a
good morning. On hearing of the appointment at the cathedral she asserts that "they" are goading K. He knows it. On a
quite prosaic level Leni's assertion and K.'s confirmation
could mean that the bank and its manager, who by now is
supposedly at least somewhat aware of K.'s deteriorating
work performance, have assigned him the unwelcome chore
of serving as the Italian's guide in order to goad K., to induce
him to improve his professional competence. On a more
recondite level "they" could be the Court. They could be
both the bank and the Court.

   Why does the Italian fail to appear at the cathedral as
agreed? What does the priest mean with his ambiguous am-
plification of his assertion that K. was the man he was seeking: "I had you summoned here"? Summoned to the side
pulpit by the verger? Or summoned to the cathedral by the
Italian, or for the Italian? The Italian, in any case, the bank's
friend, is the agent by whose offices, passive or active, K. is
brought into climactic contact with the Court's priest.

   Apparently Kafka had in mind writing several chapters
to follow "In the Cathedral" before the brief concluding
chapter, "The End." And yet "In the Cathedral" serves as a
highly effective and suspenseful penultimate chapter. K.'s
worlds are coming together, K.'s world is collapsing on itself.
Darkness and ambiguously redeeming light bridge the end
of the parable with K.'s anxious desire to quit the cathedral.
The man from the country, about to die, does not know
whether the world is darkening about him or his eyes are
only deceiving him, but in his darkness he descries a radi-
ance streaming from the door of the Law. K., trying to find

his way out of the storm-darkened cathedral, perceives the glimmer of the silver image of some saint, which, however, is instantly lost in the darkness again. "The End" occurs on a dark night.

It is the eve of K's thirty-first birthday — so that exactly one year, less several hours, has elapsed from the moment of his arrest at Frau Grubach's. As with the arrest and the warders who effected it, K. is quite uninformed about the visit of his executioners — although he does happen to be dressed in black, awaiting other, unidentified visitors. Kafka deflects the danger of excessive melodrama, while retaining a forthright enough melodramatic situation, by first inducing the reader to speculate about the other visitors who will arrive to find K. gone, but more importantly, by presenting the executioners as though they were "tenth-rate actors" — K's phrase — who had wandered in from some provincial theater. Fat and pallid, adorned in top hats, they are not very adroit about anything except plunging a butcher knife into K's heart after having walked him to a quarry at the edge of town. Even as to who shall handle the weapon, they do an Alphonse-and-Gaston act.

Not only is the night dark and the street dark as the fatal walk begins, but almost all the windows on the other side of the street are dark, many of them with curtains drawn — a picture certain to remind the reader of all the blinds habitually drawn in the buildings on the cathedral square, and likely to reinforce one's sense that "In the Cathedral" constitutes a fitting next-to-last chapter. At the most accessible symbolic level, all those dark windows with curtains and blinds drawn suggest that mankind is not terribly interested in being around to witness the last moments of K's life as an accused. The pervasive darkness also sets up — again as in "In the Cathedral" — the prominence of contrasting illumination of uncertain source and significance. Thus just before the knife thrust, K's eyes, fixed on the top story of a nearby house, register a flicker, as of a light going on. The shutters are flung open and a faintly discerned human figure stretches forward. Is it one person? K. wonders. Or mankind? Is help at hand? Whatever the answers, the careful reader notes that no light actually goes on; it is the shutters that flicker as they fly open.

Even as the portly hit men prepare K. for the knife, Kafka sees to it that humor is not absent, although in this instance it is not vaudeville — or Yiddish theater — humor, but macabre and suggestive humor, linking structurally with a motif introduced in the very first chapter. There the warders, in their zeal to appropriate some of K.'s clothing, had noted that it would otherwise just have to be handed over to the Court's clothing depot. Now, in the moonlit — more light in darkness — quarry, one of the executioners removes K.'s coat, vest, and shirt. He folds "the clothes carefully together, as if they were likely to be used again at some time, although perhaps not immediately" (284). That is, after some shelf time in the Court's clothing depot.

If the clothing depot — as well as, of course, the Court — is a constant, what is to be said of K. as a constant? Or has he perhaps undergone development during his year of ordeal? And if not development — except in the sense that he has been worn down, his energies have waned — if he has not undergone development, then does he experience an epiphany in "The End"? I find it difficult to be convinced of much development, but on the eve of his thirty-first birthday K. does seem to experience a partial or qualified epiphany.

On the walk that ends in the quarry — is that the original destination of the killers or are they just getting tired? — K., observing to himself that he won't need what strength remains to him for much longer, determines on resistance, in the manner of flies that struggle to escape from flypaper until their legs are torn off. And then he catches sight of

Fräulein Bürstner approaching the square. Or maybe it is not she, but the resemblance, as K. thinks of it, is close enough. Whether it is really Fräulein Bürstner is of little moment to K. What is important to him is that at the sight of the figure that may, or may not, have been Fräulein Bürstner, he realizes the futility of resistance. He does not want to forget the lesson she brings to his mind: "to keep my intelligence calm and analytical to the end" (282). There follows a mea culpa as well as a resolution to show that he *has* learned something from his yearlong trial.

While K.'s thinking here, if belated, is unexceptionable, even laudable, one still is obliged to harbor some reservation based on the uncertainty of its catalyst. Of course K.'s dismissive unconcern about whether it was Fräulein Bürstner or not has to be seen in light of the reality that he is, quite literally, on his death march. The result, however, seems as much irony as epiphany, thus an ironic epiphany. In another sense, his eagerness to assert to himself, thus presumably to persuade himself, that he *has* learned something, his concern, above all, that people, after he has gone, have the correct idea of his change — that is merely pitiable.

While his assigned executioners do their Alphonse-and-Gaston routine with the butcher knife over K.'s head, passing the weapon back and forth, it dawns on K. that he is expected to seize the knife and do the deed himself. More dubious enlightenment in the dark. As a consequence of the long attrition of his energies, however, he fails to rise to the occasion, to muster the necessary resolve; he merely gazes about. Although he has not previously consulted God in his travails, or even thought about God, not even in the cathedral, K. somewhat unadmirably — especially for a man who has just experienced a, let us say, qualified epiphany — lays at God's door the responsibility for his own failure to act: "The responsibility for this last failure of his lay with him who had not left him the remnant of strength necessary for the deed"

(285). Then follows the flicker of light on the shutters, the vague figure at the window, K.'s oblique invocation of the judge whom he had never seen, of the higher Court to which he had never penetrated, and finally his raised hands, with fingers spread wide, in what might, or might not, be a prayer. Kafka evidently wanted K.'s possibly prayerlike attitude to be ambiguous, for he did not incorporate here the sentence from his original draft, "I lift up my hands," with its distinctly religious ring.

The warrant for irony at the end — in fact, throughout — is far more persuasive than that for a religious, above all, a Christian *Trial*. It is certainly warrantable as well to consider Kafka's autobiographical relationship to his previous fictions and their protagonists and to recall that he wrote *The Trial* in the immediate aftermath of his first broken engagement to Felice Bauer — broken because he could not prospectively reconcile the demands of marriage with the demands of his writing. There are ample indications that he felt guilty about the break, not the least of which are that he remained in touch and later became engaged to her again.

But while Kafka knew his Freud, it would be very limiting — excessively reductive — to characterize *The Trial* as the literary result of its author's guilt feelings. If, however, one is prepared to amplify and extend a sense of personal guilt into an encompassing existential guilt, then one is equipped to interpret *The Trial* with some satisfaction. Of course — and here paradox enters — existential guilt and original sin are nicely compatible, and Christianity is bound up with the latter.

It seems a grave misemphasis, a teleological interpretation that gets out on very thin ice, to make Kafka a Socialist reformer writing a novel for the purpose of social reform — an epigonic Naturalist in terms of German literary history. It is true that he was on the fringes of a Czech youth group dedicated to reforms, but it is also true that he remained on

the fringes. It is also a fact that he was enough of an enlightened bourgeois to be extremely sympathetic with the victims of capitalistic exploitiveness as he saw them—in his
case primarily victims of industrial accidents—within the
context of his insurance investigations. It is supremely
true—it is pointless to deny it—that the bourgeois-proletari-
an dichotomy informs *The Trial*—except that Kafka does not
use the term proletarian. A proletarian atmosphere dominates the regions of the Court, but the point is, it is not
thematically fundamental. Fundamental is the plight of an
individual bourgeois, Josef K. If he is forced into contention
with an organization that thrives in the districts of the poor
and whose representatives—at least those of the lower levels,
for he never penetrates higher—are also of the lower classes,
K.'s real struggle throughout is with himself, an individual. It
is the fate of that individual to which Kafka consistently
directs the reader's attention.

   The Trial is rich in paradox, of which an imputable
Christian interpretation may be the most ironic. But the
most basic, and hardly less ironic, so obvious it is easily
forgettable, is that K. is both guilty and innocent. By the
same token he both fails to receive justice and receives justice. If he is innocent by the lights of a regular court, he is
guilty by the lights of a different Court—which is itself a
lower Court. The ending is closed: K. dies, in his own words,
"like a dog." Yet it is open in the sense that he was perhaps,
although probably not, redeemed. (One gravitates to religious terminology for a finale that may be blasphemous but
is more likely simply nonreligious, despite the belated and
abrupt introduction of God.) The dreamlike irrationalities
are real, and they are not questioned. The distortions reveal
as they conceal the empirical truth.

   The Court is distinctly K.'s adversary, yet K. and the
Court share a symbiotic relationship, in which the Court
echoes or reflects what is going on in K.'s mind. Both part-

ners in the limited-term symbiosis are characterized by ambiguity. The obligation of Josef K. to look within himself, to all appearances so obtusely ignored for so long, must nevertheless have been acceded to in small increments as his energies erode and forsake him. Does his epiphany presume such subliminal smoothing of the way? But again, is it even an epiphany?

The Trial is episodic. As in *Amerika*, characters enter, only to disappear and never return, or return only briefly. Issues, subordinate themes — for example, K.'s childhood under the guardianship of his uncle — are alluded to, even briefly raised, never to be further developed. Still, with what justice may a novel that its author never prepared for publication be called episodic? Even in its present form, it is more closely structured than many critics will grant, with a network of motifs and stylistic integrators. However much the present penultimate chapter's direct and obvious structural anticipation of the last chapter is owing to Max Brod's arrangement of the text he had at his disposal, the last chapter is clearly the last, and in a persuasive array of details it is a mirror image of the first — down to and including the pair of relentless but humorously awkward minions of the Court who are sensitive to such an apparently eclectic trifle as the machinations of the Court's clothing depot. While sexual violence — or at any rate violent sex — appears to be the norm, there is, surprisingly enough, little actual nonsexual violence: the whipping and the execution. Each evokes reference to a dog. In the former, the shrieks are passed off by K. as only a dog howling in the courtyard. In the latter, as the knife does its work, K. dies, shamefully in his view, "like a dog." The latter dog, of course, does not howl.

5

"In the Penal Colony," "A Country Doctor," "An Old Manuscript," "Building the Great Wall of China," "A Report for an Academy"

From a purely narrative point of view "In the Penal Colony," written in 1914 during the composition of *The Trial*, is distinct from most of Kafka's fiction in two respects. First, the locale is not Prague; rather it is maritime and tropical. One may think of the model of Devil's Island, although the details of the story make the scene seem more like a military outpost than a prison camp. Kafka manages also to put an unusual distance between the events narrated and the principal narrative point of view, that of the renowned explorer who visits the penal colony and witnesses an unusual and aborted execution of an equally unusual death sentence. Or rather, a sentence and a would-be execution that would be unusual elsewhere; in the remote prison colony the sentence and mode of fulfillment survive as the heritage of "the old commandant," a heritage barely tolerated by his more easygoing successor.

While the locale and the coolly distanced narrative point of view are perhaps unexpected, the question of judgment and judge — for the operator of the increasingly out-of-order execution machine is also the officer who pronounces summary judgment on the accused—the focal question of judgment places the story within the familiar precincts of Kafka's fictional concern with judgment and guilt.

The execution to be witnessed by the renowned foreign explorer is that of a simple, animal-like soldier, whose offense stands in no reasonable relationship to the capital sentence imposed by the officer. The officer, the last visible adherent of the old commandant and his summary methods of jurisprudence and punishment, takes an adherent's interest in demonstrating the workings of the horrible execution machine to the originally uninterested explorer—who, if he were so inclined, just might win the new commandant over to a retention of the machine.

Before the victims of the machine's prolonged executions at last give up the ghost at the twelve-hour mark, their sentence inscribed into their flesh by the apparatus, they experience transfiguration. That is, in the officer's view, they arrive at an insight into their transgression and their sentence even though they have not previously been aware of either. In the case of the present condemned soldier, however, because the explorer declines to promise support of these methods before the new commandant, the execution is halted in midprocess, the condemned man is removed from the awful apparatus, and the officer submits himself to its execution. Instead of exquisite torture and transfiguration, though, the facial expression on his corpse reveals nothing special. The visiting explorer, his distance from these proceedings perhaps greater than ever, can hardly wait—especially after he reads the tombstone of the *old* commandant—to get back to his ship.

During the officer's long and tendentious explanation to the explorer while the officer prepares the machine for the man he condemned, it emerges that in its present state the machine is a far cry from its glory days when the old commandant ruled and huge throngs turned out for the spectacle, to be enlightened by its macabre work. No audience for the execution shows up anymore, not even the new commandant, and the machine itself lacks proper maintenance and replacement parts. Things go wrong with some frequency, although the officer knows the machine so well that in many instances he can improvise quick repairs. A badly worn cogwheel, creaking dreadfully, is the most obvious sign of the machine's decrepitude.

The disparity between the offense of the condemned man and his capital sentence is grotesque. Every hour on the hour during the night he was to wake up and salute the door of his captain. At two o'clock one morning he failed to wake up. When the captain lashed him in the face with his riding whip, the failed sentry, rather than begging pardon, seized the captain's legs and commanded him to throw the whip away or suffer being eaten alive. The reader is reminded of the student in *The Trial* snapping at K. with his teeth. Indeed, the stupid soldier is early on compared to a dog responsive to a whistle signaling his own execution. However cruel his fate—to be killed while having "HONOR THY SUPERIORS!" needled into his body by the machine—he is not exactly a sympathetic character. As to his absurd sentence, he has not had the benefit of understanding the charge, of offering a defense, or even of knowing his sentence. As the officer explains to the visiting explorer, guilt is never to be doubted. Instinctively the reader recalls the Court before which Josef K. was accused—but the condemned in "In the Penal Colony" seems even unlikelier than Josef K. to be capable of looking within himself.

With the unfortunate—but suddenly spared—condemned man moved from the killing machine, to be replaced voluntarily by the officer himself, the machine proves capable of starting itself even though the officer in the execution bed cannot reach the starter. Moreover, thanks to his painstaking preparation of his beloved machine, it manages to run for a while without the ominous creaking of the faulty cogwheel. Soon enough, however, the entire gear assembly disintegrates—it requires nowhere near twelve hours for the officer's sentence to be performed on himself. And on the face of his corpse there is no sign of the promised transfigurative redemption.

Knowing something of Kafka's life and perhaps especially of his relationship with his father, the reader may be inclined to continue to see reflections of the paternal relationship in "In the Penal Colony." One is inevitably cued by the command, "HONOR THY SUPERIORS!" And the regimen of the old, but now dead commandant is suggestive of a harsh paternal regimen in the eyes of an oversensitive son.

"In the Penal Colony" contains also a considerable sexual component, not unmixed with echoes of sadism or perhaps masochism. The victim is placed in a part of the machine called The Bed, which is made to quiver mechanically. A part called The Harrow, mounted on a steel band described as now limp, now rigid, hovers above until it descends to effect with its embedded needles the penetration of the quivering body beneath—which in twelve hours will be a dead body.

The officer, who himself has tucked two fine ladies' handkerchiefs under the collar of his decidedly nontropical uniform, repeatedly refers with unhappiness to the new commandant "and his ladies." The commandant's ladies, for example, are said to have stuffed the condemned man with sugar candy before he was led off to execution. The commandant's ladies will undoubtedly influence his interpretation of the explorer's statements about local justice and sentencing. The commandant's ladies sit in his box seat with him at the administrative conferences that he allegedly has turned into public spectacles. And so on, in an invidious tone. The implication is: whereas the old commandant presided over a vigorous, masculine, tough, no-nonsense penal colony in which ran the writ of the old style of justice, the new commandant, surrounded by his ladies, runs a flaccid administrative apparatus in which the old style of justice is increasingly subject to question and to inadequate support as a prelude to eventual complete abandonment. The officer himself is not immune to the new atmosphere, however much he despises it. In a sense, the two ladies' handkerchiefs soaking up the macho sweat under his collar confirm his softening and predict his abdication and even his self-execution.

While the officer thus bridges the two administrations of the colony and, unsympathetically to be sure, grasps the sense of the second as well as the first, the visiting explorer enjoys no such versatility. When the officer extracts from his wallet his most valued possession, the former commandant's drawings of the execution machine—how to build it—the explorer is quite unable to read them. Not only is he of a different country, a foreignness he emphasizes as a dimension of his dissociation from the legal and penal practices of his host country, but he is of a different era as well.

Between the social classes represented by the explorer and the officer on the one hand and the condemned man and his guard on the other yawns a wider social chasm than one is apt to encounter in Kafka's Prague fiction. The condemned, a soldier himself after all, as well as his soldier guard, are coarse and animal-like (the dog simile is appropriate). A fair inference is that this is what the system has done to them, but if that is one of Kafka's points it is a minor one.

The chief themes seem to be two, one already well-known from the novels and stories, one relatively new but of noteworthy occurrence in later works. The first is the question of justice, or injustice, as it impinges on humans burdened by an existential guilt. Among the guilty are both the would-be and the actual victims of the machine, both the inarticulate soldier and the officer, as both judge and executioner. The officer as the heir of the old commandant is quite likely an anachronism—which directs us to the second principal theme: the old times, tough and righteous, are being supplanted by a new order of questionable vigor, of excessive softness, of dubious value. Assigning an apparently positive value to the rule of the old commandant and the efforts of his heir to keep the old standard intact introduces a powerful tension between theme and narrative structure.

Finally, "In the Penal Colony" may be read as a thought-provoking fragmentary parallel to the crucifixion of Christ, in which the execution machine serves as the analogue of the cross. Some would say a parody of the crucifixion, but for that there would seem to be a lack of sufficiently specific connecting detail. Most importantly, there is no resurrection of the nondivine individual from the "crucifixion" by Kafka's execution machine. There is, however, something like a cave—a cavernous space open to the road, site of a tea-house, and under a table near the back wall lies the grave of the old commandant, whose headstone contains a long inscription, reading in part: "There is a prophecy that after a certain number of years the commandant will rise again and lead his adherents from this house to recover the colony" (226).

To the extent that one is willing to believe—and one has no reason not to, except for cultural repugnance—the officer's word that previous victims have been transfigured, redeemed, through extreme suffering in the toils of the machine, one can draw a contrast between the need of redemptive suffering and the thematic softness of modern civilization. This will in turn suggest that Kafka was aware of Nietzsche's view of pain as teacher. If pain is necessary to the realization of guilt—an abstraction from *The Trial* as well as "In the Penal Colony"—then it seems likely that Kafka is taking Nietzsche at his word, or at the least is paralleling his word.

Kafka's use of the impersonal narrator or the impersonal narrative perspective, represented by the visiting explorer in "In the Penal Colony," reaches an apogee in that tale, thereafter to be gradually abandoned in favor of a more-personalized narrative perspective whose attitudes are more consonant with those of the protagonist. Such a shift necessarily entails a loss of the tension that informed the relationship between the explorer and the officer. With a compatible personalized narrator or perspective, narrative direction in general may be technically less subtle, but there is a corresponding gain in psychological complexity as the narrative point of view is increasingly within or extremely close to the protagonist rather than external to him.

The reader may sense the difference in "A Country Doctor," one of a host of stories that Kafka wrote in a creative outburst in 1917. Even before writing "In the Penal Colony" in 1914 he had been declared exempt from military service in the Austro-Hungarian army in World War I. In the same year he finally moved out of his parents' home. By mid-1917 he and Felice Bauer became reengaged. In September of that year he was diagnosed as having tuberculosis. Believing, incorrectly, that he was near death, he sent a collection of stories off to the publisher Kurt Wolff despite his typical concern that his work was not what he wanted it to be. Wolff published the collection of fourteen stories under the overall title, A Country Doctor. Some of the stories are very brief, sketches of one page; others, such as the title story, run to several pages.

If much of Kafka's fiction has the quality of dream about it, "A Country Doctor" gives more the impression of a nightmare. The doctor, whose horse has just died in the icy winter, is suddenly confronted with two splendid horses emerging from the pigsty, which has been uninhabited for the past year. He will after all be able to undertake an urgent journey through the blizzard to a patient ten miles distant. Along with the powerful horses emerges also a groom, previously unknown to the doctor. But not a groom who will accompany the doctor on his mission, rather one who insists on remaining at home in order to have his will with the servant-girl Rosa. The doctor alone, sped by dreamlike compression of time, accomplishes his obligatory trip in an instant, as if the patient's farmyard were just next door.

The patient, a young boy, is at first diagnosed as merely malingering, despite his whispered assurance that he wants to die. On examination a few moments later, however, he proves to have a fantastic rose-red wound near his right hip. No real rose, no real wound ever looked like this: granulated, clotted, suffused with small-legged worms wriggling their way out toward the light. Lying, the doctor asserts that the wound is not so bad. His nightmare horses, having pushed the windows open to look in on the scene, are ready for the doctor's "escape." But this time it is not a speedy journey. With his horses laboring at a snail's pace through the snowy wastes, he may never reach home—where the groom is assaulting Rosa. And the night bell to which the doctor had responded—it was a false alarm. Possibly, it was really false, thus at once certifying and negating the nightmare; possibly it was false in the thematic sense that the call was for a case beyond the doctor's powers. Having abandoned its priests, the world expects the doctor to be ominpotent. The theme then is recognizably similar to that of "In the Penal Colony": this age is worse than the preceding, more-vigorous, more-effective age. Redemption is not to be found—least of all in the misguided efforts of the new commander of the penal colony or the new priest-figure who is a mere doctor.

One forms one's judgment of the new commander on the basis of the hearsay denunciation on the part of the disgruntled lame-duck officer. The country doctor is his own narrative witness—indeed the story is recounted in the first person. Perhaps no prosecutor in a malpractice suit could more effectively denounce this medical minister of the new order than does the doctor himself. He is a flawed Samaritan, and he knows it but too painfully.

Or perhaps primarily a perplexed Samaritan—"I was in great perplexity",[1] he begins his story—and his perplexity in the face of an overwhelmingly difficult situation becomes his flaw. Shall he, in a word, try to save Rosa from the groom or shall he minister to his dying—as he eventually admits—patient? Once he is on his charitable mission his thoughts repeatedly return to Rosa and her unhappy fate. But in fact, to get his charitable mission launched, with the indispensable aid of the groom, he is prepared to turn Rosa over to the latter's ungentle attentions. As soon as the groom gets close to Rosa, while he is harnessing the unearthly horses, he bites her viciously, in a way that again reminds the reader of the student Bertold's biting K. in *The Trial*—a violent gesture with pronounced sexual overtones. The doctor furiously threatens to take his whip to the groom to keep him under control, but then quite consciously reflects how dependent he is on this same groom—whose demeanor betrays his awareness of his power. Rosa is the price the doctor pays. His subsequent laments may be seen as the workings of the conscience of a fundamentally decent man unable to prevail in a supremely difficult situation.

To categorize, satisfied lust has prevailed over futile charity. It is tempting, but only very slightly rewarding, to suggest that the groom's assault on Rosa, present and projected, has stimulated the doctor to a human awareness previously stifled by his professional, and maybe social, point of view. All the time—for years, he says—that this helpful and pretty girl has lived in his house he has hardly noticed her. Now that it is too late and he has failed his obligation to save her from the terror of her, and his, presentiment of what awaits her underneath the groom—Kafka's language is that specific—he seems to rue his past indifference.

The name Rosa—in German the word means "pink"—links the doctor's two chief preoccupations, for the wound in the side of his young patient is pink in color. As in English, the German adjective also suggests the flower, and the boy's wound is also roselike in conformation. But before the doctor is informed of the wound he hastily pronounces (in his haste to return to Rosa?) the boy a healthy malingerer. Perhaps the reader of *The Trial* has already sensed that something is likely to be seriously amiss in the present sickroom, for the air there is so oppressive as to be unbreathable. (The doctor's desire to thrust open a window yields to the now greater urgency of examining his patient—later, with inevitably humorous effect, the horses open the windows!)

The doctor's unarticulated wish to avoid his official and professional duty and return to Rosa is countered in a highly effectual and symbolic way by the patient's parents and a number of guests who have appeared in the sickroom. A school choir with the teacher at the head stands in front of the house singing a verse that directs the removal of the doctor's clothes as a prelude to healing; and if his healing arts should fail, he is to be killed. The family and the village elders do indeed strip the doctor's clothes off and lay him in bed with the patient, next to the awful wound. In only a slightly transformed sense, then, the doctor is unmasked, revealed, to himself as well as others, and put to applying his healing arts in a way that characterizes more primitive societies—not unmixed with sexual innuendo, in this case further suggested by the boy's flowerlike wound.

The patient is hostile, asserting that he would like to scratch the doctor's eyes out, the doctor apologetic, confessing that the present situation is not an easy one for him either. Scarcely content with this quasi-apology, the boy nonetheless knows that he has to endure that and worse. His fine wound, as he phrases it, is "his sole endowment." A description in such terms amounts to an invitation, not to say a command, to interpret the nature of his problematic wound, his endowment. Probably, like that of King Anfortas in the Parsifal legend—although in a less specifically testing fashion—it may be construed as the mark of humanity, the human condition, which the doctor, the contemporary soul saver, is unprepared to treat.

For he only tries to alleviate his patient's concerns by declaring that the wound is not so bad, especially if the boy will take a broader view of things. The doctor's naked return home has a nightmare humor about it. But because the doctor never will reach home there is nothing funny in his contemplation of his successor robbing him. For the groom, raging in his house, has Rosa as his victim. Of himself the doctor laments, "Betrayed! Betrayed!" Not only by the groom, but in the first instance by the night bell that has summoned him to his journey, the false alarm. Even more fundamentally, by his own incapacity for coping with the perplexities foisted on him by this unhappy age.

"A Country Doctor" is really not so unambiguously subject to interpretation as the above may suggest—far from it. The reader will be tempted, quite justifiably, to read it also as a parable of Kafka's own existence as seen by Kafka. Or, proceeding from the pronounced dreamlike quality of the tale, one may approach it in the light of psychosexual dream interpretation. Sexual innuendo is frequent, and the repugnant groom is a fitting embodiment of a too-long suppressed id. That in fact is a staple of the numerous Freudian critiques, except that it is often put rather more reductively: the groom *is* the doctor's id. That remains a useful and not very complicated ad hoc formulation. But matters become much more difficult when one attempts to align a Freudian *system* onto the tale—without reducing its constituents to mere mechanical keys to a presumed puzzle.

Interpretation in terms of Christianity, on the other hand, is more likely to be simply farfetched. The boy's wound may to some suggest the wounds of Christ; but as with other human victims in Kafka's writings, his redemption is conspicuously absent. Further militating against, or certainly exercising a check against a religious interpretation, is the fact that the prime symbol, the wound, is more a philosophical construct than a real wound, despite—perhaps owing to—the terrible graphicness with which it is depicted. On the whole it seems preferable—as it usually is in the case of Kafka—not to proceed reductively but, with some awareness of the implications, to accept the ambiguity as constitutive.

In "An Old Manuscript" the inferential plea for the strong and the active and the competent—for what was, formerly—is by no means so forceful as "In the Penal Colony" or even in "A Country Doctor." Nomads from the north, skilled swordsmen and horsemen, have set up camp on the square before the emperor's palace, on the periphery of which the local artisans and tradesmen have their shops. Despite the shopkeepers' efforts, the square has become filthy, literally a stable, and the shopkeepers are less and less willing to risk the hooves of the wild horses or the whips of the nomads. The emperor's guards have withdrawn to safety behind barred windows, and the Emperor himself is almost never seen at his outer windows.

The nomads are confirmed as barbarians by their war games, by their screeching, incomprehensible speech (as of jackdaws: *kavka* = "jackdaw" in Czech), their thievery, and their—and their horses'—preference for meat, even live meat, eaten while still on the hoof. While the reader is surely amused at Kafka's working the basis of his surname into the narration, the immediate plight of the shopkeepers is not so amusing—or the slightly less immediate plight of the empire, which has turned over its defense to those same shopkeepers. The point is—clearly stated—that the shopkeepers "are not equal to such a task,"[2] any more than the similarly sorely beset country doctor was equal to *his* task.

Rather than suggest that Kafka is pointing to the imminent dissolution of the nationality-wracked Austro-Hungarian Empire, complete with a persona of Emperor Franz Joseph in a rare appearance at an outer window of his palace, it seems more fruitful to suggest that the imperial model lay at hand for the thematic reprise of contemporary insufficiency. That is, the defection of the imperial guard to the safety of their barred retreat has cast the shopkeepers into a perplexity—restore order or get killed or wounded—that will soon prove ruinous for all of the potential victims: emperor, guards, and shopkeepers alike. Surely they are all guilty, not just the cowardly guardsmen.

Somewhat in the same vein as the use of the jackdaw simile for the speech of the nomads, Kafka, the vegetarian, devotes a full one-third of this little tale to the eating habits—crude, gluttonous, and carnivorous—of the nomads. At the end of their orgy with a live ox they lie about like drunkards around an empty cask while the narrator—a personalized and compatible narrator—lies hidden in the back of his shop under a pile of clothing, rugs, and pillows. His self-concealment is like that of Georg Bendemann's father in "The Judgment" before his surge to dominance. But in the case of "An Old Manuscript" the reader is very far from imagining that the shopkeepers will surge to dominance over the meat-eating nomads.

The fierce nomads from the north appear also in "Building the Great Wall of China." They are indeed the reason—the ostensible reason—that the wall needs to be built. But perhaps curiously—certainly so from the point of view of military defense—the high command has decreed that the wall be built in contiguous thousand-yard increments, each requiring five years to complete. What would result would be a porous defense, for it might well contain gaps at completion. The narrator, a reflective, subtle Chinese scholar, recommends nonetheless that one should try only up to a certain point to comprehend the decrees of the high command. Beyond that point further meditation is to be avoided. In the narrator's belief the high command has existed for all eternity, and likewise the decision to build the wall. Thus, one reasons, the merely ostensible role of the nomads. And thus quite likely the piecemeal construction of the wall. For that mode of construction, geared to the rotation of work gangs and periodic furloughs at home, conduces more to esprit than to an airtight defense of the empire.

The narrator is from the southeast, and it is the distance, the vastness of the empire that preserves the southeast from the northern nomads. However much the idea of joyous building is thematic to the tale, the construction of the wall is not narratively central but is a lead-in to the narrating scholar's discussion of the ramifications of vastness. The southeast is so far from the capital at Peking that the people do not know the name of the reigning emperor. They hardly know the name of the dynasty. The empire itself is an obscure institution. History and time bypass these people, who are eager to obliterate the present. One observes at this conclusion that cause and effect have become indistinguishable.

Again, as in "An Old Manuscript," the model of the far-flung and disintegrating Hapsburg empire is suggestive but not thematic. The obliteration of the present as a prime, popular, unifying influence — best not undermined, the scholar recommends — is possibly to be regarded as a function of vastness of any sort, even vast work. If Kafka in this instance seems to have abandoned his more typical individual focus, the tale embraces also a parable, "An Imperial Message," that reiterates the centrifugal effect — both spatial and temporal — of vastness, but with a more typical individual focus, the tripartite one of dying emperor, indefatigable but perhaps nonarriving messenger, and "you."

Kafka's later animal stories — predominantly from the 1920s — are anticipated by "A Report for an Academy"(1917). The report is submitted by one Red Peter, an ape who has learned to make his way in the world of humans as a highly successful vaudeville artist. The members of the Academy have requested an account of the life that Red Peter former-ly led as an ape, but he explains that the door to his ape past is now virtually closed, that he could never have achieved his present successful integration had he been so stubborn as to cling to his origins. In giving up being stubborn, so as to find his way as a human, he has had to pay the price of a defi-cient memory of his apehood. Not, evidently, a price that he regrets in the slightest — and in any case, he regales the members of the Academy with ample biographical details and reflections dating from after his capture on Africa's Gold Coast.

The situation is made for irony, for mordant observa-tions on humankind — Red Peter "managed to reach the cul-tural level of an average European"[3] — and Kafka takes full advantage of the opportunity he has created. Red Peter in-curred two shot wounds on being captured, one a slight wound in the cheek, one made by a "wanton shot" appar-ently in his private parts. He now has a disconcerting predi-lection for taking down his trousers to show visitors where the shot entered, evincing an unconcern asserted by wind-bag commentators to be evidence that his ape nature is not yet completely under control.

Disdaining the desperate remedy of escaping his cage on board ship off the coast of Africa, only to end up in the embrace of neighboring pythons or of the deep sea over-board, Red Peter distinguishes between the sublime disillu-sionment of freedom — freedom that perhaps had been barely possible in the ape world — and the more practical "way out," in whichever direction; he opts decidedly for the latter. Thus: imitate humans; learn, learn, learn. Especially learn to drink; conquer your revulsion and learn to drink (does he also privately savor the counterfeit illusion provided by drink?). Of the two possible fates awaiting him on arrival in Hamburg: another, bigger cage in the zoo, or the vaudeville stage, the latter he correctly perceives as his "way out." By dint of superhuman self-discipline and dedication, he rises to the pinnacle of the entertainment profession, of the art that constitutes the way out of an otherwise intolerable plight. In such summary phraseology, one recognizes the parallel or perhaps even the bond between Kafka and his fictional ape. Hardly less than Gregor Samsa or Georg Bendemann, Red Peter is a persona of his author.

But there is a level of paradox and of humor here untouched in the earlier stories. It of course resides in the animal nature of the protagonist who claims, probably honestly, that he no longer can effect a connection with past apehood, no more than can any of the gentlemen of the Academy. It is still necessary, however, to understand — conceivably the same would as well be true of the learned gentlemen of the Academy: that Red Peter does *not* become human. He learns to act as if he were human. He does not think matters out in a human way; influenced by his human environment — in the first instance members of the ship's crew — he acts as if he were thinking matters out in the human way. His bent for exhibitionism, as he correctly implies, is not a relic of apehood but rather another facet, like drinking, like striving, of comporting himself — acting — in the human fashion. When his long and active day is done, Red Peter returns home to a little half-trained female chimpanzee, from whom he takes comfort "as apes do." In her eye is "the insane look of the bewildered half-broken animal" (184). Only he, no one else, sees it, and he cannot bear it. That is to say, she will soon be acting more like a human.

6

The Castle

Kafka began writing *The Castle* in January 1922. In September of the same year he abandoned it, still unfinished. In the fact of its incompleteness, it is thus like *Amerika* and *The Trial*. It is unlike them in that it seems more nearly to approach completeness and that it embodies a greater degree of integration. Kafka is revealed as a much more magisterial novelist now than was the author of *Amerika* and *The Trial*.

It would be easy, perhaps facile, to say that he is an author now matured by life and by impending death. Four and a half years have passed since his tuberculosis was diagnosed; he had become familiar with the world of the sanatorium and with the prospect of early death. He had retired from his insurance post. Heartbroken for a while at the departure—of course instigated by him—of Felice Bauer from his life after the breaking of their second engagement, he had fallen in love with, even become engaged to, another girl, Julie Wohryzek. That engagement broken, he had fallen in love with a married woman, Milena Jesenská, his Czech translator. Since Jesenská would not leave her husband—although she had overwhelming cause to—Kafka in his relationship with her was spared the anguish of the marriage-writing dichotomy that had previously cast its shadow so threateningly—or at the least, ambiguously. Perhaps also the edge was softer, the boundary between love and writing was less abrupt, because Milena Jesenská had an appreciative sense of what Kafka was doing as a writer — as well as of his no small ability to express his ideas in Czech as well as German. Although biographical interpretation *is* generally valid for Kafka's fiction, seeing Jesenská and her cruel and thoughtless husband as the prototypes of the fictional characters Frieda and Klamm in *The Castle* — as some critics incline to do — amounts to a simplistic and self-limiting view.

Like *Amerika*, like *The Trial, The Castle* is not a roman à clef, but a novel featuring an autobiographical hero on a quest — ultimately for justice. Unlike the quests of Karl Rossmann and Josef K., however, that of the present hero, K. — the significant initial is his only name — is more active than reactive. He seeks unbidden — or at any rate dubiously bidden — to establish a connection with the castle, to penetrate to the castle itself through the buffering maze of its self-protective bureaucracy, and to force it to confirm the legitimacy of its bid to him, his presence in its neighborhood, and his claim on its assistance. Indeed, what strikes one quickly about K., the land surveyor, in contrast to both Karl Rossmann and Josef K., is his greater forcefulness, one may even say aggressiveness. The castle, the Law, the transcendental force does not come to him, he comes to it. As befits a confrontation with a castle, he practically assaults it — not in storming its ramparts (actually it has none) but in incessantly pushing, pushing, pushing for it to recognize his presence, to take him into account in ways satisfactory to him. He is a resilient besieger, but the castle, with all the defensive and offensive wiles of an impersonal and entrenched bureaucracy, is no less a formidable adversary. The exquisite — the crueler for that — bureaucracy is Kafka's symbol or metaphor for the unattainable, like the Court in *The Trial*.

K. assertively presents himself as the land surveyor whom the count of the castle is expecting. His timing is doubtful — late in the evening — and the place is wrong — the village beneath the castle — because it is too late to present himself at the castle. He arrives on foot, in deep snow, with neither the instruments nor the assistants necessary for him to ply his trade. As if these details do not already cast doubt on his authenticity — or, more precisely, his authenticity in relation to the castle — his very appellation itself, Land Surveyor (or rather the original German for that name) is an invitation to the reader to question that authenticity. The first component of the word *Landvermesser* is obvious. And *-messer* relates to a person who measures or a thing that measures (thus, also, *Messer* as "knife"). But *vermessen* as a verb has to do with the striking of presumptuous and arrogant poses, as well as with surveying. It may repay the reader to keep these inherent connotations of the German word elements in mind as he or she follows the contest of the land surveyor named K. with the castle (German *Schloss*, which also means "lock," inherently embraces the verbal sense "to close, to close out, to exclude").

The initial telephone calls to the castle placed by its representative at the inn do not bode well for the travel-weary but hardly reticent land surveyor. The reaction to these initial calls reflects the castle's resistance to contact, let alone penetration and granting of unambiguous recognition. Recognized finally, ambiguously, and reluctantly, he may be; but as for permission to proceed to the castle . . . And he is tired, tired and drowsy as he tries to sleep in a makeshift sack by the stove — for there is no room at the inn. His fatigue will prove thematic: almost at the end of the novel, almost at the point of a rapport — a possible rapport — with a possibly appropriate castle bureaucrat, K. is overcome by such accumulated fatigue and sleepiness that he cannot respond, dozing off during a possibly — but one never is certain — propitious interview.

The Castle as a well-integrated novel does not replicate *Amerika* and *The Trial* in having themes introduced never to be developed, and characters brought forward rarely or never to be seen or heard of again. K.'s fatigue vis-à-vis his castellar adversary, or its minions, is predictive and thematic: he is finally to be worn down and apparently defeated. So it is in his relationship with the antagonistic village schoolmaster when K. finds no possibility of serving in the role of surveyor for which he avers he was originally engaged. So also his early meeting in a peasant home with some of the idiosyncratic, no less antagonistic peasantry; they will re-emerge in his life, more fully identified, their idiosyncrasies more linked to their backgrounds, their antagonism perhaps ever so slightly muted. Fundamentally, however, as the schoolmaster advises him, "there is no difference between the peasantry and the Castle,"[1] a maxim that K. seems ever in danger of forgetting, to his disadvantage.

Of the greatest importance to K.—and to reappear throughout the novel—are his assistants, his assistants-to-be, whom he meets in the village street as they come down from the direction of the castle. The first meeting is brief, just in passing, as Arthur and Jeremiah, laughing, dressed in the tight-fitting clothes worn by the employees of the castle, announce that they are headed for the inn—the inn at which K. is at least temporarily quartered. K. at this point does not know that Arthur and Jeremiah have been assigned as his assistants nor, for that matter, that their clothing signifies their association with the castle.

The castle itself dominates the village on which it looks down. It is a rambling pile, neither old nor new, apparently comprised of numerous small buildings. K. can espy only one tower, about which wheel masses of crows—hardly an auspicious omen. Curiously, whereas the village lies under snow as high as the cottage windows—K. has already got bogged down once—the castle, as far as he can see, is almost entirely free of snow, just limned by a thin layer that defines it all the more clearly in the glittering air.

The snow that half-buries the village is not the result of

any single severe storm. One gains the sense that the snow is a virtually yearlong characteristic of the village. It seems that it has always just snowed or is snowing. Snow, and adapting to it, define the physical terms of life in the village — and probably more than merely the physical terms. Spring and summer are exceedingly brief, hardly known. Cold, ice, and snow are the norm, with all that that implies as to conditions of life as well as attitude toward life on the part of the villagers.

It is also just about all there is of nature in *The Castle* — perhaps the more significant for that reason. As always, it is internal landscapes that Kafka is interested in, his characters ever turning inward, on themselves and on each other. It has been critically suggested that the castle and the village comprise a landscape of death that K. has come to. Certainly there are many details — the half-buried village, the crows, the almost endless winter — that support this possibility. "Short days, short days," says K. to himself on returning to the inn, noting with surprise that darkness has already set in, although he has been gone, he feels, only an hour or two, and he is moreover not hungry. Whether or not the landscape is one of death, the related foreshortening of time, so pervasive in Kafka and so striking in *The Castle*, is indeed a dream characteristic. One is surely well advised, as with many of Kafka's earlier works, to consider *The Castle* throughout in terms of dream narration, illogical, suggestive, symbolic.

Back at the inn, K. is again greeted by Arthur and Jeremiah, who now present themselves as his assistants. On K.'s asking if they are his old assistants, they reply affirmatively, adding that they have come a long way — even though it has been just from the castle. All of this is most peculiar, although maybe less so when considered in the light of dream narration — and/or in the light of K.'s own authenticity. The questions are obvious: Is K., who never practices surveying within the compass of the novel, in fact the surveyor he claims to be? Or is he presumptuously posing? Has he received a commission from the castle as he claims? Or has he just happened in, as sometimes is suggested, at the conclusion of a journey from a long way off? How is it that he cannot identify his old assistants, cannot tell whether the new ones are the same as the old ones? To these questions there are never any clear answers.

It may be that K. is simply bad at identifying people. He professes inability to distinguish *between* the two new assistants (quite aside from their putative identity with his old assistants), declaring that Arthur and Jeremiah are as alike as two snakes — a surely ominous suggestion. So indistinguishable (to him) are they that he proposes to call them both Arthur and orders that they are to function as a single entity. So much for K.'s ability to relate to individuals. If he perhaps enlists one's sympathy in his quest to break the castle's defenses, one's sympathy may be tempered by the realization that K. is not a humanly sympathetic hero — he uses people. In his fashion he is as impenetrable as the castle.

Informed by his old-new assistants — who may remind the reader of the warders in *The Trial* — that no stranger can get into the castle without a permit, he has them telephone the castle. The no in response is audible even to K. at some distance from the instrument; "neither tomorrow nor at any other time." Going to the telephone himself, he hears a buzz the like of which he has never heard on a phone before, "like the hum of countless children's voices," or rather the echo of voices singing at an infinite distance, "trying to penetrate beyond mere hearing" (26–27). Impenetrability appears to be endemic. Even when an official's voice comes on, it reveals a small defect in its speech, although K., posing as one of his own assistants, has no difficulty in recognizing the word "never."

Whom K. will next use, with the castle's cooperation, is

the messenger Barnabas. Barnabas, whose biblical namesake came to figure as an apostle and whose name means "Son of Consolation," is a self-appointed messenger, hoping in this role eventually to repair the wretchedness of his family, which has incurred the disfavor of the castle. K.'s use of people, perhaps especially of Barnabas, is not free of a disagreeable social snobbery — as in patronizingly ordering beer for Barnabas on realizing again that the clean-cut and responsible youth is after all only a messenger. This snobbery, however genuine, should not be permitted to mask or diffuse the outlines of K.'s even more unappealing habit of regarding people as objects to be manipulated and exploited. Yet at other moments one is encouraged to think of K. as a sensitive person in comparison, for example, with the castle functionaries.

From the castle Barnabas brings a letter to K. that ambiguously recognizes K.'s appointment while at the same time demeaning his uncertain role — as, say, K. demeans that of Barnabas. In effect K. has the option of becoming a village worker with a merely apparent connection with the castle or, on the other hand, an ostensible village worker whose real occupation is determined by the castle through the medium of Barnabas. K., who may already have forgotten the schoolmaster's maxim of nondifferentiation between peasantry and castle, unhesitatingly chooses the former.

Although the signature to K.'s letter of entitlement is illegible, Barnabas tells him that it belongs to a department chief named Klamm. The surname is suggestive. While one has to discount the connotations of English "clam," one may regain them almost completely by invoking the German adjective *klamm*, meaning "tight, hemmed in," or the Latin adverb *clam*, "secretly." The name additionally evokes — indeed is identical in form with — the past-tense form of the archaic German verb, *klimmen*, "to climb." Klamm, the castle bureaucrat in charge of K.'s case, is, to say the least, a highly private, that is, inaccessible person; and one can hardly doubt his ambition in having risen to his present post, although now, ensconced in a department headship, he is reported to sleep much of the time. At any rate his inaccessibility is merely typical of the castle bureaucrat caste. As the landlord of the Herrenhof, the village inn reserved for those bureaucrats, assures K. in the process of forbidding him access to facilities other than the bar, all of the "castle gentlemen" are so sensitive that they could hardly stand the sight of a stranger.

K. has already met Barnabas's two strapping blonde sisters, Olga and Amalia, as well as their senile and invalid parents, who present a tableau of uncomfortable humor in their snail-like slowness in advancing to meet K. Humor in *The Castle* is typified by this doddering pair, cruelly destroyed by the castle in their prime. The novel contains more than a few humorous episodes — burlesque essentially — but the humor tends to be cruel. That is true even of the humor directed back onto K. himself — for example, his getting mired in the snow in his unwise venture off the main street, or in his marathon lovemaking with Frieda the barmaid on the barroom floor of the Herrenhof, rolling around among the puddles of beer and other refuse. It's funny, to be sure, but one also feels a certain disquiet at the spectacle — and this before one perhaps fully realizes that the lovemaking is in fact, from K.'s side above all, exploitive lovemaking.

K. and Frieda (German *Friede*, "peace") are in a very real sense made for each other. She is coquettish, in a not entirely spontaneous way, but still her personality seems ill suited to the imperious impersonality of the bureaucrat Klamm, whose mistress she is. When Klamm calls her in his impersonal fashion from his room adjacent to the bar, it is never quite clear whether he wants beer or sex, which probably helps make Frieda, already discontented and annoyed about many aspects of her life, open to the possibility of a liaison with K. Frieda, who started as a stable-girl at the Bridge Inn, is a striver and by striving — and not wholly by Klamm's influence — has advanced to the considerable eminence of barmaid and even shows promise as a future manager. She scorns the peasants and their crudities — including Olga and the entire Barnabas family, because of whom she may to a degree be motivated to "rescue" K. She disdains not less the servants of such castle functionaries as Klamm, actually contemptible peasants whose beer glasses she is obliged to fill. And whom, when they become too objectionably raucous, she drives from the barroom with the aid of a whip.

K. is obviously a striver too. And despite his exploitive motive he is anything but impersonal in his conquest of Frieda. Conquest is hardly the term. With one desire they sink into embrace and remain thus for hours. Kafka's language here, especially so when the erotic ambiance consists of puddles of beer, is devastatingly satiric: "hours in which they breathed as one, in which their hearts beat as one, hours in which K. was haunted by the feeling that he was losing himself or wandering into a strange country, farther than ever man had wandered before" (54).

The language above, amounting to a satire on the centuries-old European love-story genre, now finally made obsolete by a story like that of K. and Frieda, is all the more satirically effective because it is also the language of fantasy fulfillment — two becoming one — as well as of desperately craving certainty amidst alienation. There is nothing very edifying about either the physical or spiritual union of Frieda and K. For her, the risk of discovery — if it is a risk — is outweighed by the possibility of even strengthening her position as barmaid. Desiring salvation by way of Klamm's recognition, K. loves Frieda just so long as she may be useful in helping him obtain — hardly *at*tain — that salvation.

When during the perfervid — perhaps perfervid because desperate — lovemaking Klamm calls for Frieda, K. only too dutifully repeats the summons of her paramour into the impassioned Frieda's ear as he helpfully refastens her blouse. "I'm with the Land-Surveyor!" (55), Frieda shouts to Klamm, beating on his door, near to which she and K. have rolled. K. is distraught, Frieda has betrayed everything. That is, in K.'s opinion, by spurning Klamm she has threatened her position as Klamm's mistress. It is only as Klamm's mistress that she can be of value to K. Put still more crassly, Frieda is worth more to K. as Klamm's mistress than as K.'s lover. That is not a very auspicious basis for a marriage between K. and Frieda.

True, before K. marries her he counts on having a talk with Klamm and, even more promptly, with the mayor, who is designated as K.'s immediate superior in his letter of entitlement signed (illegibly) by Klamm. Frieda is not alone in citing the impossibility of an interview with Klamm; she is backed up aggressively by her friend and former employer, the landlady of the Bridge Inn, a formidable woman with an implacable hatred of K. and disdain for his ignorance — as a stranger — of the way things are done in the village. The landlady's hatred is brought into sharper focus by two emotional considerations: first, K. is going to marry "our dear little Frieda," with whatever that portends for the relationship of the villagers with Klamm and the castle; and second, K. socializes with the family of Barnabas, pariahs in the village, even brazenly noting that he can take advantage of their hospitality should the landlady kick him out of the makeshift maids' quarters that he occupies at the inn. For K. does not yet know — nor does the reader — what sins the family of Barnabas has committed.

Chapter 15, devoted to these sins and their retribution, is an anomaly within the structure of the novel, a subdivided chapter twice as long as any other and four times as long as the average. Kafka doubtless would not have allowed the imbalance to stand had he prepared the novel for publication. At present chapter 15 seems to call attention to itself too much for an excursus that has little to do with K. direct-ly — although it is instructive as an extended parable of the irrefragable domination of the village by the castle.

The Barnabas family's sins — not unlike K.'s, externally considered — consist in their being outsiders vis-à-vis the cas-tle, and thus pariahs in the village-peasant society, which is bound up with the castle. The family of Barnabas did not reach their pariah state more or less automatically — or exis-tentially — as did K., by virtue of being strangers from a long way off, ignorant of the society dominated by the castle. They reached it — and came to their ever-more desperate and futile and condemned attempts to repair it — by virtue of failing to respond to a castle signal that should have been, and probably was, well-known to them. In short — by now quite the opposite tack from that taken by the obsequious K. — at a fatal moment they had the temerity to defy the castle quite openly.

What motivated their daughter Amalia to reject the lewd proposals contained in the letter from the castle official Sortini? — not to be confused with Sordini, the bureaucratic workhorse who tracked down the confusing background of K.'s appointment, or perhaps nonappointment. Sortini — with a *t* — notices Amalia at a fire brigade picnic and is smit-ten, though not in a very honorable way. Amalia, who knows the rules of the game as played by the castle and its people, nevertheless chooses to ignore them. Like K., but without obsequiousness, she spurns the dominance of the castle. In so doing, she reveals her outraged sense of decency and personal worth, with perhaps an admixture of self-right-eousness. In fact, in a distorted shifting of values brought about by the castle's and Sortini's expectation, Amalia could even be described as selfish, for in the preservation of her own decency and in the absence of any feeling of guilt, she condemns her family to ruin. Not that the castle visits anything overt on the doomed family. Its members are merely shunned, ostracized, deprived of a livelihood, and by their own attempts to recoup their fortunes made to look — and be — ridiculous and pitiful.

With the sudden descent of Amalia's and Olga's and Barnabas's parents into senescence and decrepitude, Barnabas, castle messenger and occasional cobbler, becomes, despite his youth, the head and support of the beleaguered family. It can hardly be by chance that it is Barnabas whom the castle assigns as messenger between the castle and K., thus assuring K.'s association with the outcast family and his consequent contamination in the eyes of the village, to the substantial disadvantage of his quest to attain to the castle.

The long, subdivided chapter 15 serves also to focus what the reader has probably sensed throughout as an aura of lewdness surrounding and emanating from the castle, and penetrating into the village. It is neither so specific nor so schematic as the seductions or quasi-seductions in *Amerika* and *The Trial*. Nor, as in those novels, does it involve primarily women as the more active seducers. (Before Frieda, probably many mistresses before, it was the present landlady of the Bridge Inn, Gardena, who had been summoned to Klamm. Three times — then his whim evidently turned elsewhere.) True, this last generality appears to conflict with Frieda's teasing, highly overt sexuality. But the point here is the deeper one that the castle, in the person of the impersonal Klamm, has already enlisted Frieda in the role of sex object; the reader can either regard her ready lovemaking with K. as an extension of that role or, more empathetically, as a personal revolution against it. But the repeated equation and association of coitus and beer — spilled, stale beer — seem to reflect the castle's fundamental yet trivial lewdness quite as well as Sortini's sudden lust upon seeing Amalia.

If K.'s call on the mayor, his nominal superior, fails to enlighten him in the details of the Barnabas family sin —

Amalia's refusal—it does afford him a further insight into the bureaucratic workings of the castle, expecially as bearing on his own status, which, as the mayor too often reminds him, is the most insignificant of all petty matters. Further deflating K., the mayor, who like many a Kafka impresario operates out of a sickbed, interprets his letter of entitlement from Klamm to be meaningless from an official point of view. K. barely rescues his cherished letter from the mayor's wife, who has folded it into a paper boat. She, aided by K.'s ubiquitous assistants, has in any case failed to turn up any entry whatever in the mayor's overflowing files, in the category "Land-Surveyor." A nonperson in an invalid nonposition, K. will be fortunate to be relegated to some lowly makework job in the bureaucracy even as he continues to crave access to the highest, unattainable reaches. He can't simply leave, retrace his long road here. Because, castellar ambition aside—but maybe not very far aside—he is going to marry a local girl. A local girl who has already been obliged to relinquish her prestigious position as barmaid at the Herrenhof.

K.'s further official—and qualitatively more official—enlightenment as to the realities of his relationship with the castle is provided by Klamm's village secretary. This is Momus, named after the son of Night, and the faultfinder par excellence in Greek mythology. If Barnabas has offered cheerful hope and the mayor a blundering absence of either hope or hopelessness, the hearing conducted by Momus, egged on by the antagonistic landlady, Gardena, is calculated to disabuse K. of any remaining shred of hope. On the other hand, in ironic and bewildering contrast is the second letter from Klamm, full of praise for K.'s surveying (which he hasn't done), encouraging continuation of the work—and recommending calm confidence.

Not entirely unlike the country doctor's horses out of a pigsty, fate, in this case the bureaucracy, provides for K. and Frieda a means to an end. They are hired at starvation wages as live-in custodians of the two-room schoolhouse—and virtual slaves of the tyrannical schoolmaster. This is a long, fruitless, excruciating byway, made more hazardous, here as on every step of the way, by the antics of the assistants assigned to K. by the castle. Arthur and Jeremiah are both antic and malevolent, both young and old, both innocent and worldly-wise, both loyal and disloyal—because their first loyalty is naturally to the castle. If K. imagines that Klamm, with whom he has in common not only the experience of Frieda's affection but also the significant initial of his name, is going to become more accessible to him through the offices of these "assistants," he does not entertain that illusion for long. He is essentially on his own in that quest. Frieda, to be sure, does allow him the use of a private peephole giving to the room that Klamm frequents near the barroom at the Herrenhof, and Klamm is visible, sitting at the table—even if asleep, as Frieda later assures K. K.'s later attempt to accost Klamm as the latter departs the Herrenhof by sleigh comes to naught, almost to fiasco.

Indeed there is something fiascolike, almost grotesque, in all of K.'s attempts to make contact with the castle, or even to improvise an existence for himself and Frieda in between these misguided if perhaps logical attempts at contact. The existence as live-in custodians, out of synchronization with the goals and schedules of the schoolmaster and the teacher, bedeviled by the assistants, approaches burlesque. There is a basic incommensurability between what is going on and what is desired: a morass of petty personal incomprehensions and meannesses rather than the achievement of K.'s exalted—and probably sadly overrated—goal. Although K. knows well enough that Frieda accounts for at least her own share of the popular antipathy toward the family of Barnabas, he nonetheless lingers at the Barnabas house overlong, manages a ludicrous backyard-fence escape when tracked down by Jeremiah, only to learn that Frieda is

abandoning him, perhaps for Jeremiah, certainly for rein-
statement as barmaid at the Herrenhof.

If they had only gone away somewhere that first night,
Frieda laments to K. — before returning to the room she now
shares with Jeremiah — then everything would be different
now. Perhaps. But go away is precisely what K. could not
and cannot do. He has to stay and try to fulfill his self-
imposed transcendent mission. Frieda has more than once
hinted that as an insider, a villager with a close relationship
to Klamm, she takes a more distanced view of the castle and
its works, a view that cannot be realized by the outsider K.
On that ground alone, one suspects, she will enjoy a more-
compatible and less-tempestuous relationship with Jeremiah.

The first German edition of *The Castle*, as well as the
English version based on that edition, comes to an end at
the conclusion of chapter 18. The later fourth edition adds
two chapters that impart more of a sense of completion,
although not, it must be added, a very subtle or convincing
conclusion, for the added chapters seem to reflect only partial integration with what has preceded. K. is afflicted with
fatigue, of which there has not been much mention of late;
and his overwhelming fatigue is responsible for the failure of
what may have possibly been his most successful attempt to
attain to the castle. Possibly — but on the other hand perhaps
not.

Barnabas has reported that one of Klamm's chief secretaries, Erlanger by name, wishes K. to report to him in room
15 of the Herrenhof when Erlanger conducts his usual night
office hours. The name of this chief secretary, to the extent
that Kafka is not indulging in irony, suggests that K. is at last
on a promising track, to the extent that any track could be
promising for him. The verb *erlangen* means "to achieve,
attain." K., however, is so tired that he botches the appointment.

At four in the morning, in search of an empty bed as much as anything else, he blunders into the room of a liaison secretary — not one of Klamm's — named Bürgel, who invites him to stay and chat. As to K.'s appointment with Erlanger, Bürgel suggests that toward five o'clock people begin to get up and that is when K. is apt to have the best success in responding to the summons from Erlanger. Bürgel's name appears to derive from the verb *bürgen*, " to vouch for, guarantee," so that both K. and the reader may be inclined toward a positive anticipation. Perhaps especially so on Bürgel's announcement that he transacts most of his business, his correspondence as well as his interviews while in bed — and during the daytime too. In this preference for conducting business from bed one recognizes the potentially ironic tableau of the busy professional according to Kafka. But also the incompetent, overburdened professional, such as the village mayor.

Bürgel, genial, almost tireless talker that he is, is yet a dilettante, K. realizes, in grandly offering, despite his evident ignorance of the case, to do something leading toward K.'s employment within his job classification. Or is he? He *seems* to be offering the possibility of a breakthrough. In the course of a tidal wave of the most tedious, disquisitional bureaucratese, which would surely have put to sleep even an attentively wide-awake person, let alone the already fitfully sleeping and dreaming K., Bürgel asks: "What sort of oddly and quite specially constituted, small, skillful grain would such an applicant have to be in order to slip through the incomparable sieve [the castle bureaucracy]? You think it cannot happen at all? You are right, it cannot happen at all. But some night — for who can vouch for everything? — it *does* happen" [Emphasis on *doch* is Kafka's](317). Is Bürgel, in all his long-winded tediousness, offering a miracle that K. is too sleepy and too incredulous to believe? Or is Kafka offering more satire (of which conceivably K.'s incredulity is also a part)? Whichever; K. is sleepily impervious to either miracle or satire.

Almost impervious as well to the summons of Erlanger, who happens to be in the adjoining room, unable to sleep owing to the noise of Bürgel's voice. K. staggers into the next room, to be reproached by Erlanger for his tardiness. But that is the least of it. Through Erlanger K. is brought to the most precise awareness yet of the futility of all his endeavors relating to the castle, thus to his quest for transcendence. This perhaps climactic insight is provided by Erlanger's almost casual but significant iteration of the possible disturbing effect on Klamm — but of course Klamm is not susceptible to disturbance in the usual sense! — of the presence of a new barmaid. In a word, Frieda must be brought back to replace Pepi, a former chambermaid who was installed as her successor when Frieda left to join K. Erlanger's hint that K.'s cooperation in this "trivial" matter may be of advantage in his aspirations is all it takes now to make K. see the light, or at least part of the light. Never mind that Frieda has in any case already left him.

The remainder of K.'s illumination is less an epiphany that a cumulative realization. After his abrupt dismissal by Erlanger he remains in the corridor of the inn watching the early-morning distribution of files from a cart to the various rooms in which each of the castle secretaries awaits the files assigned to him. But the servant attending to the distribution is manifestly angry at K., the castle secretaries hardly open their doors — which makes reassignment of files and corrections of misassignment most difficult and confusing — and one secretary is screaming, shouting, and ringing a buzzer. Why all the hubbub? Because K. is an interloper here, he has no business lingering here after his interview, he is allowed only in the barroom: in his fatigue, almost like intoxication, he has acted ignorantly. Ignorance, the bane of the outsider who doesn't belong. His ignorance, his guilt, is both specific and existential. He is reproached by the landlord and the landlady; at first he cannot understand for what. And for a long while he cannot get any answer. His guilt was routinely inferred by both of them, who hardly imagined that K. was asking in good faith.

If the reader is looking for an equally summary narrative detail, it is doubtless to be found in the single small piece of paper left in the file cart. It is the last and surely least file, not allocated, or at any rate not distributed, for action. K. has the uncomfortable feeling that it is his own. The servant in charge of the cart, silently admonishing his assistant to silence at this unique irregularity, tears the paper to shreds and puts the pieces into his pocket.

The final, twentieth chapter is mostly an epilogue consisting of the story of Pepi, Frieda's replacement as barmaid for four days. If one has heretofore entertained a sympathetic view of Frieda—probably the reader has absorbed some of K.'s apparent admiration if not his infatuation—Pepi's perspective, however controlled by her jealousy and frustration, is a powerful corrective, both as to Frieda's physical appearance and her character. Pepi, not incorrectly, attributes her own rise to barmaid to K., and as well blames him for her fall. Because it was K. who wooed Frieda away from her post and it was he who couldn't hold her, who allowed her to gravitate back to the barmaid post, which is hers, Frieda's, if she wishes to resume it.

But in Pepi's mind—perhaps in fact—there is more. In her reconstruction of background and events, Frieda as barmaid and as Klamm's mistress had, by her very appearance and character, many disadvantages. She had to worry all the time about growing indifference toward her, by the customers, by Klamm. She had to provide a spectacle of some sort, cause a scandal in order to remain a viable barmaid and mistress. She needed a coup. She decided upon an affair.

And K., unknown and unknowing, that is, ignorant, proves the ideal respondent.

In thus taking a more exacting look at Frieda through Pepi's eyes one will wish to avoid idealizing Pepi—for which there is little textual warrant. (The name Pepi is a diminutive form of Josephine, apparently a favorite name-base of Kafka, as in Josef K.) Pepi may be younger than Frieda but she is hardly more attractive, she has even poorer taste, she is sentimental, and in her ambitiousness too insecure, too contentious, too eager to please. As to the traits proceeding from her ambitiousness—cruelly aborted by her forced abdication as barmaid—Pepi is not unlike an exaggerated version of K. himself, a similarity that the latter, evidently now more keenly aware of personal nuance than on his first entry into the village, specifically recognizes.

Pepi's version has the advantage of making K.'s affair—his quest, so to speak—with Frieda an analogue of his quest for the castle. A stranger from far off, ignorant, is attracted to an object—sex object or castle—assaults it tempestuously but perhaps not without plan, and in the longer run the object proves elusive. Of course, if the analogy holds, it runs both ways, and if Frieda is really unattractive, then so is the castle. Why did Frieda leave him? K. wonders in response to Pepi's tale, and comes up with the answer that her defection was probably owing to his neglect, a conclusion amply supported in the text. That would appear to suggest, following the analogical principle, that neglect as well is the most advisable course of action toward the castle. Although K. reproaches Pepi for her "wild imagination," it may be worthwhile for the reader—not to mention K.—to take her version of matters with some seriousness and to draw the quasiconclusion: disregard the castle, which in any case is not what it seems or purports to be. Perhaps that is what K. is about. Is that the gist of his implication that he will join the chambermaids in the cozy, insulated little room in the bowels of the Herrenhof? Of course such an implication has a sexual component, whether or not primary. In any event Freudian critics will see in it a symbol of K.'s wish to return to the womb—certainly tantamount to turning away from the castle.

The Herrenhof is still forbidden territory to him—he is permitted only in the bar—and he will have to be careful to keep his cover. He will presumably help the chambermaids with some of their work, which Pepi has lamented is too heavy for girls. It is not unreasonable to imagine that a sexual relationship will develop between K. and Pepi. But this is speculation beyond the compass of the novel, as is his possible future desistance from trying to connect with the castle, which is still there. So also, presumably, is K.'s need—however obscured by weariness—to penetrate it and wring from it an acknowledgment of his claim. He seems an unlikely person to forget it all and simply settle down to crude peasant existence in the icy, half-buried village.

Earlier critics, doubtless to the gratification of Max Brod, and including Thomas Mann, author of an homage incorporated in the commonly available American paperback edition, were given to interpreting *The Castle* as an extended religious allegory. (They may have been encouraged by the fact that the proper names in the fiction are plainly allegorical.) According to such an interpretation the castle, the transcendent entity that K. aims to penetrate and persuade of his "rights," represents God. Perhaps the granting of rights rather than the adjuration to rightness is the appropriate business of this presumed God, who (or which) would seem to give the essential impression of being fickle, fearsome, and obscene. Not that man's religions have necessarily eschewed such gods, but the evidence of the text simply does not avow much in the way of divinity.

In the absence of textual hints it seems advisable to

abandon the notion that the castle somehow represents God. The castle has too many un-Godlike features — to those noted above could be added pettiness, inefficiency, and error-proneness — for any coherent divine picture to take shape behind its after all not very prepossessing walls. The castle is the castle. It is perhaps as recondite and illogical as many a god, it may even be an obstacle *to* God, though no particular stress is laid on that possibility.

As the castle seems not to represent any recognizable Godhead, so K.'s quest does not represent a religious pilgrimage, which hardly ever finds the pilgrim contentiously and probably calculatingly — K.'s affair with Frieda — seeking his rights. As if it were not already invalid by reason of deficient motive, the pilgrimage interpretation disintegrates completely on consideration of the fact that the relationship between the quester and the goal, K. and the castle, does not appreciably change during the course of the novel.

Far from having embarked on a pilgrimage, K. exhibits practically no sense of guilt, not moral, not existential, least of all religious. Wherever he is from — a long way off is all that one knows — he is on a rational quest to define and assert his status and his rights, as he construes them, to be beset by delay, by nonsense, by stupidity, malevolence, ambiguity — and even some ambiguous benevolence. How very different is his response from the episodic, irrational, and guilt-laden struggles of Karl Rossmann and Josef K.!

While Kafka could hardly help drawing on his firsthand knowledge of the Austro-Hungarian bureaucracy, of which he was himself a part, *The Castle* is much more than a grandiose satire of bureaucracy, or even an allegory of bureaucracy as the life in microcosm of twentieth-century man. The castle bureaucracy is simply that — nothing else is required to amplify its deadly resistance to K.'s rational purpose — a part of the castle and a part of the whole novel.

Kafka was well versed in the works of the early Freud,

but it does the artist, and the reader as well, a disservice to imagine that *The Castle* is a psychiatric case study of a neurotic patient named K., a structure that an earlier generation of critics was wont to impose. Reductive criticism, whether religious, sociological, or psychological, is easy, concerning itself with only the conveniently amenable portions of the whole. Especially in the case of a masterwork like *The Castle*, the reader-critic is apt to gain the most not by restricting his critical focus, but by making it embracing and comprehensive — even ambiguous — as is the work itself. There is no key to *The Castle*. There are a number of perspectives.

7

"Investigations of a Dog," "The Burrow," "A Hunger Artist," "Josephine the Singer"

Kafka's stories from the 1920s—the majority of them employing animals in the central autobiographical and/or narrative role—seem to reveal a somewhat more accepting spirit than do most of the earlier tales. It is easy to assign this shift to Kafka's having come completely to terms with his own mortality as a result of his tuberculosis. But yet, if one is dealing with an author as quintessentially autobiographical as Kafka, it is probably not inappropriate to invoke this circular critical standard. The later tales with an animal as the authorial metaphor (or the counterpole to the author-figure) do indeed seem more accepting, more resigned, not less ironic but perhaps less savagely ironic. It could be fairly said that "A Report for an Academy" (1917) is savagely ironic. "Investigations of a Dog" (1922), given its title by Max Brod, is more quietly, almost—but not quite—whimsically ironic.

Of considerable length—forty-six pages—this fragment has received less critical attention than one would suppose. That may be so because it is as much meditation as story and, at first glance, seems to run to wordiness. But the wordiness, the inner contradictions, the exquisite ramifications are of a piece with the consuming—quietly consuming—

irony of the whole. The canine hero, like most of Kafka's heroes a figure easily identified with the author, narrates and meditates in the first person. If the dog were a human — but he rigorously excludes any contemplation, or even recognition, of humans — one would say that he figures as the center of a stream-of-consciousness narration.

But he — he has no name, which would after all be one bestowed by humans — is no introspective sophisticate. His reflections, for all their sometimes-labored complexity, are those of an innocent, himself on the fringes of dogdom, to which he protests — too much — his devotion, his sense of togetherness. Although nuances are necessarily sacrificed, and one should moreover be on guard against the temptation to impose a symbology, it may be helpful to compare this reflective canine outsider to a human artist vis-à-vis his surrounding society — say a human artist like Kafka. Analogously the dog, thence Kafka and the reader, is concerned with the tortured and unsolvable problem of individuation within the mass. Or — and here the symbolic leap lacks any textual suggestion — the narrator, author, and reader are concerned, from a typically German or Central European standpoint, with the plight of the twentieth-century European intellectual in an industrializing world.

These are serious matters to be addressed by the conceit — of course not original with Kafka — of a speaking, or rather a writing dog, for the hero is not participating in a dialogue, he is for the most part his own interlocutor. Certainly this narrative situation provides opportunity for the exercise of wit on the foibles of dogs, some of whose preoccupations are a staple of human humor, but Kafka's canine humor is light and suggestive rather than obtrusive. He endows his reflective innocent with dignity and with zest — if dubiously directed zest — in the pursuit of his metaphysical investigations into the basis of his own existence, however inclined one may be to smile at the unsoundness of the dog's research methodology.

For this reflective dog, blinded by patriotism for his canine race, is incapable of recognizing the human race and thus the special and intimate symbiosis, spiritual as well as physical, between dogdom and humankind. "For what is there actually," he asks, "except our own species?"[1] The irony, as seen from the two racial points of view, is two-edged. Our hero, thrown on his own self-circumscribed resources, is at a severe disadvantage when he inquires into the question: On what does the canine race, pledged to silence and adjured to water the ground diligently that it may produce, nourish itself? "Whence does the earth procure this food it gives us?" (31). And yet food comes to dogs from above; the ground, then, attracts food vertically, also obliquely and in spirals, from above. The unknown or at any rate unacknowledged presence of humans condemns the canine researcher to continuing metaphysical error.

So disappointed finally is the dog investigator at this unsolvable — unless humans are factored in — conundrum that he resolves to fast as long as he can stand it: the fast as "the final and most potent weapon of research" (64), abstention from precisely that whose secret he is determined to solve. Far from wishing to perish, he wants to achieve truth and escape the world of falsehood. Nonetheless, he finally faints. When he comes to, he is lying in a pool of his vomited blood, and standing before him is a strange and beautiful hound, who orders the invalid researcher to leave his hunting preserve. But the invalid impatiently perceives that his savior-to-be is going to sing, and when that happens, the disembodied song induces his recovery. Perhaps his research into food, thus penetrating to the heart of dog nature, should have been blended with the science of music. That is, for an artist — if he is an artist — it would be well to concern oneself with spirituality as well as with the business of making a living.

The musical theme, rare enough in Kafka's works — one thinks primarily of the effect of Grete Samsa's violin playing — which resolves the conclusion or at least the rather formless ending as we have it of "Investigations of a Dog," has been anticipated toward the beginning of the tale, during the late puppyhood of the narrator, by the unforgettable episode of the musical dogs. Bursting forth from somewhere out of the darkness into the light are seven dogs, not speaking, not singing, but conjuring music from the empty air, and facing this music of their own making courageously and calmly. (One may imagine that they are actually members of a carnival dog act, accompanied by a human orchestra.)

In their devotion to their art, however — or to their human trainer invisible to the investigator owing either to his guilelessness or to his deliberate self-deception — the seven musical dogs commit two of the most serious offenses known to dogdom. First, they fail to greet or to reply to their investigating brother; no dog can pardon such an offense against good manners. Second, they blatantly reveal their nakedness by walking on their hind legs — an abomination! But the music they make, or seem to have made before vanishing back into the darkness, almost drives the youthful researcher out of his senses. Their concert is the turning point of his life. The memory remains for his whole life, and one finally sees, and hears, the reprise in the hunting dog's singing before the aged and weakened investigator.

After having seen and heard the seven dog musicians with his own eyes and ears, the investigative dog considers everything to be possible; his powers of apprehension, he feels, are free of all prejudice. It is thus that he is able to accord credence to reports of aerial dogs ("air-dogs," to replicate the original German; in translation they are called "soaring dogs," but they do not soar, rather they simply hover or float in the air, in extratextual reality probably being carried in the arms or on the laps of their human — and thus unseen — mistresses). Why do they float in the air? the investigator wonders, and what is the sense in their doing so, apparently detached from the nourishing earth, thus in a sense reaping without having sowed? With supreme irony, at the same time suggesting the inevitable interpretation of the role of the tiny and feeble creatures, the narrator-investigator observes: "Someone now and then refers to art and artists, but there it ends" (36). But the professional and perhaps personal parallel is probably clear to the thoughtful reader. The aerial dogs are dependent on their fellow dogs, it appears; they are perpetually talking, philosophizing. They are lazy, and their philosophy is as worthless as their observations. It is to be wondered if they have the strength to propagate.

Of course there is something not only ironic but also artistically shallow — to the extent that is not itself ironic — in handing the reader an interpretive key on a narrative platter, and it must be admitted that "Investigations of a Dog" has not fared entirely well with critics. In addition to the perhaps excessive — unless ironic — obviousness of the proffered interpretive key, the story lacks its ending — although it *does* have a resolution — and in the critical view there are long stretches of tedium in the personal and philosophical reflections of the canine narrator and hero. Perhaps. Perhaps too the charm of the tale outweighs its drawbacks. There is the delightful sense of Kafka, in the persona of the dog, discoursing on himself through a transparent mask. And not least the delight of reading a dog story in which the dog, even as he is a persona of his author, is true to his own kind, not merely a human inside a shaggy coat. In contrast to the ape Red Peter, in "A Report for an Academy," who learns to act as humans act and to act as if he were thinking in a human way, the dog researcher is dog through and through (and even if he is permitted to protest too much). Particularly rich ironic dividends are gained by the dog's rigorous, if perhaps unconscious exclusion of humankind from his purview.

While the dog in "Investigations of a Dog" is indubitably a dog, and the genus of the animal in Kafka's other stories of animals is never in doubt, the builder and inhabitant and protagonist of "The Burrow"—one of the last two stories that Kafka wrote—is without name, either generic or given. Although critics have not unanimously resisted the temptation to make guesses—a badger is the favorite—it is perhaps just as well to forgo guessing at a taxonomy that the writer did not think it advisable to impart. All the more so as the burrower is the most intensely and transparently autobiographical persona of the author himself.

The burrower, now past his prime, has in his years of vigor built himself a redoubtable burrow, complete with a false entrance, as well as a cunningly moss-covered genuine entrance, an introductory labyrinth—built before he had perfected his technique—innumerable circular rooms, a ventilation system, and near the center a magnificent castle keep. (Kafka's name for the castle keep is *Burgplatz*, the first component of which—like *Schloss*—means "castle.")

Still, life aboveground is not without attraction to the burrower, despite the greater risk of confrontation. It is here that he hunts most of his prey, which he then, often with difficulty, conveys back to the larder—or, periodically subdivided, larders—in his burrow. Only small game, intruding small fry, can be obtained underground. Not that larger beasts are absent beneath the ground, constructing their own burrows or perhaps just reconnoitering—the burrower once heard such a beast through his walls, but it went away, fortunately. Fortunately, because the burrower in his youth and confidence neglected to include practical defense works in his building, giving himself over more to a sensual delight in his burrow and a neurotic contemplation of theoretical perils. Nowadays, for example, he loves to contemplate his splendid underground castle keep from a slight distance. He would like to reemerge to the ground above and spend his life contemplating the entrance to his burrow, finding happiness in reflecting on what a superb protection the entrance would afford if he were inside.

The burrower returns to his burrow from one supraterrestrial sojourn to hear an extremely faint whistling noise through the walls of his redoubt. At first he would dismiss it as inconsequential—he ought to have liquidated the small fry more thoroughly. The noise does not vanish, however, and the burrower becomes irrationally agitated in his perceptions of how best to locate it and eradicate it: by random probing, systematic trenching—or simply ignoring it. The volume and frequency of the noise are inconstant. Its quality changes: it seems to be more like gurgling. It cannot, he finally surmises, be owing to any conceivable aggregate of small fry. Rather it must be a single huge beast burrowing its way toward him, and when it pierces the wall—even assuming that it is just wandering and not extending its domain and that mutual understanding is thinkable—there will be a baring of teeth and claws. The decisive factor will be what the adversary may know of the agitated owner of the burrow and the castle keep. It is possible that the adversary may never have heard of him, nor have actually heard his work, for he works very quietly.

The interpretation lying closest to the surface, so to speak, is the autobiographical one. Kafka is reflecting himself, as usual, in the protagonist of his tale, in this case the unnamed burrowing animal so given to neurotic reflection in his skillfully but not quite perfectly fashioned subterranean quarters. If the outside world is quite literally that beyond the burrow's moss-covered entryway, that world into which the burrower makes occasional forays, then the burrow itself may well symbolize the world of art and literature, lately threatened by an unseen, impalpable but still real adversary, which is perhaps to be understood as symbolizing Kafka's fatal tuberculosis.

The outside world is by no means unknown territory to the burrower. He knows it well, and though it seems to be a world of kill or be killed, he appreciates the advantage that the outside offers as a post for reflective contemplation of, at least, the entryway to his elaborate underground domain. It seems noteworthy that the history of this particular burrow, while rich in details of tunneling and construction and of food gathering, contains no allusion whatever to nesting, to a mate, to progeny, the perhaps normally expected tableau within a burrow. This burrow is a home and fortress, not a home and nursery.

As with many another Kafka work—"A Country Doctor" comes quickly to mind—it is possible to interpret "The Burrow," at least to a degree, as a sexual metaphor. There are hints in the original German—for the most part, however, dissipated in translation—that this is not out of the question. The burrowing or potential burrowing by an enemy would represent sexual penetration. Thus in his dreams the burrower often "see[s] a greedy muzzle sniffing round it [the dark moss of his covering] persistently." What would happen "if in his obscene lust he [his enemy] were to discover the entrance"?[2] It would seem highly reductive to assign primacy to such an interpretation. However, as an adjunct to the more persuasive and even heartrending autobiographical schema of a dying man and, perhaps, a dying artist, it is not necessarily to be dismissed as outrageous. For in the context of the sterility in the burrow, it conduces to a most plausible and effective irony—irony of the broadness that characterizes Kafka's late works.

Such irony is characteristic, above all, of "A Hunger Artist," a much more concise tale. Thus the ascetic "artist"—

the German designation, *Künstler*, in this context is no less ironically suggestive — excites, for a while, public admiration for, and suspicion of, his ability to fast for forty days. Whereas in fact — what he alone has known during his salad days of starving — starving is the easiest thing in the world for him. He can't help starving. "Why?" he is asked on his deathbed, which is the dirty straw of his cage, long forgotten by his circus employers, not to mention the customers, "why?" He replies simply that he couldn't find the food he liked; had he been able to find it he would have "made no fuss," that is, would not have starved and would have stuffed himself with food like anyone else.

The forty-day period, certainly, recalls the temptation of Christ in the wilderness and thus invites the reader down the path of religious and ethical allegory. That path, however, narrows impassably on the reader's reflecting that the hunger artist was not resisting any temptation, he was only doing what he had to do; he could do no other. And what he does hardly qualifies as ethical any more than as artistically distinctive, although, in his halcyon days of starving, it did make a handsome living for his manager even as it seemed to contribute to an ill-defined spirit of bourgeois uplift in the communities where he gave his long-running show. Irony is as abundant in these derivatives as in the fasting itself. Any critical suggestion of religious or ethical righteousness can only succumb to the pervasive irony.

The reader gains no notion of what sort of food would appeal to the artistic starver. The frequent critical notion that it is spiritual food finds no support in the text. What is certain is that the hunger artist's replacement in the circus, a sleek and hungry leopard, is fed plenty of the food that *he* likes — that is, raw flesh. The leopard too is confined in a cage, and he hardly has the option of leaving. (For that matter, neither does the hunger artist, but his compulsion is internal.) Whereas the hunger artist has performed before ever-dwindling crowds, the customers throng about the cage of his successor, reluctant to leave a spectacle that appears to celebrate the joy of life — even if it is a confined life.

As in "In the Penal Colony" and "A Country Doctor," the contrast between former times and the present seems to be a principal theme of "A Hunger Artist," and even it is accorded a more ironic treatment in the latter tale. Hardly more edifying — or less edifying — than the reign of the popular and definitely nonanorexic leopard who succeeds the hunger artist as the cynosure of popular taste, were the glory days of the hunger artist. There would seem to be very little art in the art of starving for the sake of personal satisfaction, however compulsory that satisfaction. And even less in doing so to enrich the impresario who presents the act to the public, a showmanly operation in which the hunger artist is a willing and — especially in the postfast public celebration — even duplicitous participant. That is, his hungering is genuine, he does not nosh at concealed tidbits as the spectators suspect, despite the humorously elaborate — because completely unnecessary — safeguards built into the act to guarantee probity. But he does, habitually, lend himself to stagy manipulation in the triumphant aftermaths, for example, in allowing himself to be persuasively shaken by the impresario in order to demonstrate his bodily weakness to the public. There is nothing very religious and nothing seriously artistic in this.

What it is — recourse to metaphorical or symbolic explanation is hardly needed — is show business. That is to say, the practicing of welcome deception, for profit. Kafka is not angry about it — one thinks of his enthusiastic enjoyment of the Yiddish actors in their skits of trumpery. One sees through it, enjoys, perhaps later reflects ironically. Kafka helps guarantee irony in his story by employing a personalized narrator, unnamed, characterized only by his narration, evidently a showman, a salesman in the mold of the impresario, with whom he is steadily sympathetic. On the other hand, this narrator has no entrée — how could he? — into what goes on inside the hunger artist's mind. Thus the grotesqueries, the misapprehensions about those thoughts, as well as the atmosphere of professional conning — even the hasty narrative dispatch of the remains of the unfortunate starver and the precipitate welcome to the leopard, who is capable of attracting satisfactory crowds. Paradoxically, the leopard in every sense is a healthier act. He is not likely to be so susceptible to the use of irony, nor to be interpreted as an artist — or a saint. If his bill for food is perhaps substantial, he is at least eating it himself rather than paying for overly rich breakfasts for quite superfluous overnight watchers.[3]

The last of Kafka's animal tales, indeed the last story he completed — and took the initiative himself in publishing — is "Josephine the Singer, or the Mouse Folk" (1924). Properly speaking, it is not a narration but rather a discussion by the fictive narrator, a conscientious and highly articulate fellow mouse, of the relationship between the mouse singer Josephine and the thoroughly unmusical mouse community of which she is a unique member. The discussion, replete with reflective qualifications, not to say contradictions, assumes the general tenor of showing how the unmusical mouse commonly adapts to the extremely idiosyncratic musical artist in their midst. The mouse community is nonartistic, one is given to understand, for the same reason that it has no sense of history: the demands of life, of survival amid constant worries and terror and attrition, are too overwhelming to permit either the leisure or the reflection necessary for art to bloom.

The narrator, as limited as in "A Hunger Artist," but at least not a showman, has no particular insight into Josephine's mind and motivation; he reports only what an observant and objective — but he too is a mouse — witness to her concerts would see and hear. Despite the reverence in which Josephine and her art—they are inseparable—are held, despite her assertion of the airs of a prima donna, despite her arrogance nurtured by the appreciation of her fans, and her insistence on that appreciation, the question remains: is Josephine an artist at all? For her presumed singing is in fact no more than the squeaking noise emitted by all mice without their even being conscious of making the noise. And yet Josephine has somehow parlayed this nontalent into an art acknowledged by all who assemble—who are expected to assemble—when she is in the mood to offer a concert.

On the model of "A Hunger Artist" the reader is perhaps tempted to regard Josephine's art too as under the cloud of at least partial spuriousness. What kind of art is it, to allow oneself pretentious airs while doing only what one does naturally? The difference between the art of the hunger artist and that of Josephine lies in both the production and reception of the art in question. Josephine's concerts are in no wise show business, nor is her audience comprised of spectators wishing only to witness a spectacle or, to put it even more pejoratively, wishing only to be in the swim entertainmentwise. Nor are Josephine's audiences—even if some members have been rounded up and coerced into attending by her lieutenants—likely to dwindle and vanish, leaving the artist alone. The bond between artist and community is too fundamental, too powerful. In fact, it is Josephine who ultimately vanishes, just a day or so before the discussion that is in effect her story, and just at a time when she was scheduled to give a concert. If on earlier occasions she has required to be cajoled into singing, this time her desertion is complete.

What is the effect of her desertion on the mouse community?—always the community, one hardly is aware of individuals. The community—the narrator uses the first-person plural pronoun—will get over the loss, true; but it will not be easy. It is suggested that even during her lifetime—her disappearance is evidently equated with death—Josephine's squeaking was a mere memory and that, accordingly, it was so highly esteemed that it could not be lost. In other words, as the title of the tale suggests and as the tale itself testifies, Josephine, for all her foibles, resonated to the pulse of the community. She will be exponentially redeemed in something very like the collective unconscious, forgotten yet, paradoxically and dialectically, remembered. This must be the sense, for in the same final sentence the mouse narrator reasserts that the mouse folk do not busy themselves with history.

The resonance suggested above does not, it may be helpful to reiterate, presume a sentimental or even friendly relationship between artist and audience, between individual and community. The constantly prickly relationship is brought to a head by Josephine's insistence on being exempted from the work expected of every community member, so that she may be at full strength for her concerts, which, in her style of presentation, subject her to very considerable physical and emotional demands. The desired exemption is not granted, Josephine is furious with resentment, which the community absorbs even as, anything but her enemy, it continues its devotion to her triumphant art.

Some critics, seemingly impatient of Kafka's ambiguous mode—the relationship between Josephine and the mouse community clearly is fraught with ambiguities—are concerned to impute clarity and simplicity to a work of fiction lacking those reassuring qualities, and in the bargain to mistrust the signs of humor. While it is true that the mouse cohort indulges in behavior not unlike that of humans, it seems preferable to be amused by instances of such behavior—for example, sycophancy—rather than to generalize thematically from them to emerge with a model of the human condition. By the same token, Marxist infatuation with the continuity of the presumably triumphant mouse mass (the community) at the expense of the vanished individual violates the ambiguity and the nuancing and capriciously disregards the author's own ending.

Max Brod was the first to venture the suggestion that the often beleaguered mouse community was a metaphor for the Jewish people. The chief difficulty with that is that it requires ignoring Kafka's specific and repeated disavowal of historical sense, of historical memory in the mouse community. On the whole, in the stories as well as the novels, a superior critical approach involves taking Kafka's word rather than indulging predispositions that yield interpretational tidiness at the expense of the whole work.

8

~~~~~~

The Parables

In addition to his longer stories, most of which have been discussed in the preceding pages, Kafka wrote a much-larger number of shorter stories and parables. The genre of the some fifty-five shorter pieces may in some instances be uncertain, for in a sense they are all parabolic — as indeed are all of Kafka's works. In another sense almost none, not even of the ostensible parables, is a true parable. That is, while the shorter pieces are more or less unembellished, simple in form as well as didactic in purpose, they lack explication of just what it is that is being purposefully taught by example.

No such difficulty confronts the reader (or the hearer) of a biblical parable — most prominent in the New Testament. For instance, early in Matthew 13 Jesus propounds the parable of the sower and the seed: some seeds fall by the wayside, some fall on stony places, some fall among thorns, and some fall into good ground. Then, after a clarification — also couched in parable — explaining to his disciples that to his larger audience it is not given to know the mysteries of the kingdom of heaven, Jesus quite formally elucidates the parable of the sower and the seed: The seed fallen by the wayside represents — is — anyone quite unreceptive to the Word, the seed in the stony places is a hearer who has no depth, the seed in the thornbushes is he whose preeminent concern for things of this world chokes the inchoate Word, and finally, the seed in good ground is the hearer who both hears and understands the Word and lets it bear fruit. The hearer is scarcely required to hunt for or improvise an explication; it has all been done for him, and whatever the logical risk inherent in metaphoric analogy, the hearer is content in his uncomplicated enlightenment.

A more-complex sort of satisfaction—or perhaps even dissatisfaction, frustration—awaits the reader of a Kafka parable. For he or she will encounter no step-by-step elucidation—in fact, usually no elucidation whatever. The reader will instead have the pleasure or displeasure of propounding his own or, sometimes, choosing from among the author's suggestions. And not necessarily just one; several explications may be possible, with no favorite, maybe even mutually contradictory—but all with a certain amount of textual justification. The reader will of course bring to bear what he or she knows of Kafka's background and propensities as well as, inevitably, his or her own background for reception.

The first of a representative eleven parables to be discussed here is a very-early example, contemporary with *Description of a Struggle* or "Wedding Preparations in the Country." Told in the first person, it is called "On the Tram." The narrator stands on the rear platform of the streetcar, a model of self-admitted personal insecurity and isolation. His attention is attracted to a distinctive, pretty girl preparing to get off the streetcar at the next stop. How is it, he asks himself in conclusion, that she keeps her lips closed and does not exclaim in amazement at herself? In the absence of any answer to that question as well as of any explication of the whole, the reader may infer that the narrator is overwhelmed at the girl's apparent self-confidence and relatedness to her environment, in such striking contrast to himself. There seem not to be many alternatives. One such might be the ironic possibility that the pretty girl, despite appearances, is actually as desolate as the admiring and probably envious narrator. In any case, the at least mildly perplexed reader will have probably identified — is indeed, in the use of the first person, invited to identify — the "I" with Kafka himself.

"Before the Law" is surely Kafka's best-known parable, significantly placed in chapter 9 of *The Trial*, some ten pages before Josef K. is executed. The parable had already been published by Kafka separately. As with any parable, it stands on its own, even while it is enriched by the context of the novel of which it is a thematic microcosm.

The parable is told to Josef K. by the priest in the cathedral, where K. was supposed to meet the visiting Italian businessman who, however, has failed to keep the appointment. The priest impresses K. as the one person potentially sympathetic with K.'s plight as a victim of the Court's idiosyncratic persecution. But the priest, whose parable of the man from the country and the doorkeeper is very far from easing K.'s mind, only tortures K. further by proposing, after the telling, a number of possible explications, his whole performance propelled by bursts of pedantic dialectics. None of these explications can have been of much satisfaction to K. And the explication that is not suggested, the simplest of all, would afford the least satisfaction of all.

The man from the country who wishes admittance to the Law would for at least two reasons seem to be a dolt — if a decent, trusting dolt. First, his very appellation, the man from the country, is a traditional metaphor for a dull fellow. Second, he allows himself to be dissuaded by the somewhat brutish doorkeeper from pursuing his desire to penetrate to the Law. He believes and trusts the doorkeeper's explanation that he, the doorkeeper, is only the first and mildest of a forbidding array of doorkeepers stationed at successive inner doors. The man from the country, patient and credulous, puts up with the doorkeeper's patronizing demeanor. Believing the doorkeeper's vague assurance that if permission to enter is impossible now it may be possible later, he settles in to wait for the long term.

Finally, senile and on the verge of death, the man from the country asks the doorkeeper how it comes about that no one else has craved admission; for everyone, so he asserts, strives toward the Law. Perhaps; but the doorkeeper roars at him that no one else could be admitted at this particular door, because it was meant only for the man from the country. With that he announces his intention to close it.

So much for the simple believer's trust and patience — and by parabolic extension so much for the prospect that trust and patience and decency will avail Josef K. in his uneven contest with the Court. Although the words are not spoken, "Forget it!" is what in effect the priest, the teller of the parable, is advising K. to do with his continuing protestation of innocence. The effect is extremely ironic: a priest, in a cathedral, tells a parable that lacks any coherent religious explanation or reference. In his scheme of things the meek and the humble seem unlikely to inherit very much but continued difficulty.

Other interpretations are possible. One that would find a Marxist resonance has the man from the country being adjured — but self-defeatingly and ironically too late! — to dynamism rather than static waiting. That is, he ought to have promptly burst through the door. Such a resolution, however, flies against the context of the novel (and against Kafka's outlook in general), in which the more K. struggles, the more he enmeshes himself in the toils of the Court. In the post-parable dialectics both K. and the priest find potential explication in this or that personal flaw of the petitioner or the doorkeeper. The personal flaws are obvious; their causative roles are not susceptible to clear proof. It seems preferable — since in this rare case the possibility exists — to enlist the novel as context for the parabolic explication as well as the extended object of the explication. That favors the perhaps disquieting revelation that the parable describes the typical reward for patience and trust. The implication that simplicity, widespread in both its admirable and pejorative senses, leads to gullibility and thence to deception would then be irony added to irony.

"The New Attorney"—the title is surely a tongue-in-cheek allusion to Kafka's own profession of law—is an apparently charming conceit from 1917, in which Bucephalus, the war-horse of Alexander the Great, has returned in the person of a practicing lawyer and legal scholar, a Dr. Bucephalus. No longer in the midst of clangorous battle, he somewhat reclusively devotes himself to poring over the ancient tomes in the law library. Kafka's matter-of-fact description of what is after all an anomaly, not to say a miracle, implies a modern tolerance for miracles: people have the insight to realize that Bucephalus nowadays is in a difficult situation.

By no means, however, is the contemporary attitude to the good. How different it was—and how exhilarating, it is implied—in the days of Alexander the Great, who over a banquet table could put a spear into his friend and who had the vision of reaching the gates of India, now completely unattainable in spite of all the brandishing of swords. This more-critical explication suggests that it is perhaps not modern insight but rather modern insouciance, modern softness, the lack of a grand vision, that unblinkingly indulges such an anomaly as Bucephalus in the role of attorney.

Thematically then, this humorous parable—though some critics remain unamused—echoes the less mirthful "In the Penal Colony" (1914) and "A Country Doctor" (1917). Further, such a theme cannot help but hint at a Nietzschean thread in Kafka—although the latter is hardly disposed to conceptualize a superman to restore the balance to the strong and the active as against the weak and the tolerant.

From the same year as "The New Attorney," 1917, is "The Neighbor," a sketch of similar brevity—a page or so—that seems more autobiographical than parabolic. It is told in the first person by a young businessman who sees the adjacent office suite rented to a presumed competitor, one Harras. Beset by suspicion, the narrator has no hard information on Harras. Sometimes he meets him cursorily on the stairs; Harras always has his key at the ready and slips quickly into his office. Despite his suspicion, the narrator up to this point — consistently in the present tense — has managed to retain his self-possession while discussing his new neighbor. But on his comparing the elusive Harras to a rat's tail the reader may be prepared for a lapse into neurotic obsession.

Thin walls separate the offices, and the narrator imagines Harras listening to his telephone conversations, divining the names of customers even though the narrator avoids using names while on the telephone. Acting on his eavesdropped information, Harras is imagined to rush out and steal the customers. A parabolic explication — one ought to whisper over the telephone! — seems unlikely. Rather the sketch seems to reflect Kafka's coolly coming to grips with neurotic fearfulness, which the reader sees gathering force as the tale proceeds. The ending, still in the first person, present tense, is even open, if not precisely hopeful. Such hopefulness as there is lies in the self-irony, or at least self-distancing, that informs the sketch.

"A Crossbreed," from about the same time as "The Neighbor," is more a parable, or at any rate a Kafka parable — for, typically, it lacks explication. It also lacks the extended critical attention that has been accorded many of Kafka's parables. The indefinite article in the title, as not infrequently in the parables (and not infrequently in the longer stories as well, for example, "A Country Doctor," "A Hunger Artist"), suggests at least the possibility of generalization. The narrator — perhaps one should think in terms of *a* narrator — has as a legacy from his father a curious animal, half kitten, half lamb. Sharing behavioral as well as physical characteristics from its mixed ancestry, in the sun on the window sill it purrs curled in a ball, on the meadow it gambols friskily. And like a dog it is faithful — why shouldn't it be? — often inseparable from its human companion.

Does it cry when the narrator is oppressed by problems? It does put its muzzle to his ear as if it wished to say something, gazing in his face to seek confirmation of being understood. Perhaps, the narrator speculates finally, the knife of the butcher would provide a "release" for the animal. But no, it is a legacy from his father — although it gazes at the narrator with a look of human understanding in a way that seems to challenge him to dispatch it.

It is perhaps easy to guess why critics tend to avoid "A Crossbreed." But the narrator's threefold assertion that the odd animal is a legacy from his father reminds one of Kafka's mixed legacy from his own parents and challenges the interpreter to explicate in an autobiographical direction. The two strains of Kafka's mixed legacy would be those of artist and businessman, or artist and lawyer: an artist inhabiting the too-tight skin — the animal's skin is said to be too tight for it — of a member of the family of businessman Hermann Kafka. Such a neat, specific, autobiographical explication, however, removes from "A Crossbreed" the quality of general applicability that would make it a parable. Perhaps Kafka is saying that all tormented artists should be given the release of death — is that the generalization that one seeks? Or is explication superfluous?

Like "Before the Law," "An Imperial Message" (1917) is set within a longer work, in this case the incomplete "Building the Great Wall of China," a fragment of some fifteen pages, of which the parable occupies hardly one. The fictional narrator (one knows from the larger work) is a Chinese scholar concerned to explain the relationship between the far-flung Chinese people and an extremely remote emperor.

In the parable the dying emperor carefully dispatches a message, presumably some kind of recognition, by way of a messenger to his humble subject — "you," addressed in the second person. But the physical obstacles to delivering the message are so formidable, the distance so far, and the time lag so great—millennia—that not even the most indefatigable messenger could conceivably succeed in delivering the emperor's message. However, concludes the narrator, when you are sitting by your window in the evening you can dream the message up for yourself.

Is the resolution proffered by the narrator one of weary, perhaps sentimental resignation to the familiar-enough Kafkan picture—as in "Before the Law"—of deceiving misplaced hope and trust, of fostering hope and trust only to let them go unrewarded? Or on the other hand, granted that the message remains undelivered, is the "you" to take heart from the climactic assertion—Kafka sets the last sentence off with a dash—from the assertion that you have it within you to dream up on your own the contents of the absent message? (It is worth noting that German *erträumen* lacks the somewhat automatic irony of English "dream up" or "dream to yourself.") Kafka evidently anticipates his reader's casting the explicational dilemma more or less in the above fashion, but he has no intention of resolving the ambiguity. For immediately on resuming the surrounding tale he causes his narrator to describe the burden of the enclosed parable with the paradoxical phrase, "hopeless and hopeful."

"A Little Fable," written in 1920, is indeed little (the title is Max Brod's), just seventy-six words in German, a few more in the English versions. Most are spoken in one long sentence by an increasingly panicky mouse on the run. At first it feared the world so big, but now the world is becoming smaller as the formerly distant walls converge, and now the mouse is in the last room and in the corner stands the trap that he is running into. The cat observes that the mouse need only change direction . . . and eats it up.

Numerous possible explications revolve around the concepts of power and weakness, power and fear, fear and stupidity, and fear as the cause of inflexibility; but none is apt to prove definitively enlightening and all seem to depend on extratextual uncertainties. That dependency is no less true if one chooses to see another Kafkan instance of how the world rewards hope and trust. For to cast the mouse as the bearer of hope and trust undeceived by catastrophe, one would need to make him a confidant of the cat. Evidently he *is* addressing the cat, but the degree of confidentiality is doubtful. On the other hand, the mouse's faith is implicit, and his reward—whether or not one thinks in terms of "Before the Law"—is not unexpected.

Somewhat similar is the apparent purport of "Give It Up!" (1922), although a wide range of other possibilities can be summoned up, depending on the extent and the nature of the extratextual inferences on the part of the interpreter. Given the distractions along the brief flow of the first-person narrative, one hesitates to call it simple, even compellingly simple; elegant seems a good term.

The narrator, not long in an unfamiliar city and on his way back to the railway station, notices that his watch is quite slow, compared with the tower clock. This discrepancy—he seems automatically to assume the tower clock to be correct—persuades him to hasten; in his haste his unfamiliarity with the locale becomes a crucial disadvantage. Spying a policeman, the narrator breathlessly asks directions. The policeman, smiling, mocks the query: how should *he* be expected to know the way? When the narrator insistently confesses his own incompetence in finding the way, the policeman twice counsels him, "Give it up," turning away abruptly as if he wanted to be alone with his laughter. Unlike the fatuous mouse in "A Little Fable," it appears that the narra-

tor is indulging a reasonable expectation of finding reasonable succor in a reasonable quarter. That his faith and trust
are so cruelly, even mirthfully answered—almost a satire on
his cliché predicament and cliché response to it—makes this
a more powerful parable than that of the trusting mouse,
who ought to have known better, and the hungry cat. For
the narrator has reason to know better.

Dubious explications of "Give It Up!" depend heavily
on such detailed observations as the unreasonable presence
of a policeman on a deserted street very early in the morning
(is that unreasonable?); on the clock tower as a phallic symbol; on the narrator's uncertainty (granted); on the temporal
discrepancy and the narrator's immediate assumption of
personal rather than official flaw; even on the presumption
that European railroad-station clocks (is it a railroad-station
tower?—the text does not unambiguously say so) were always reliable. It seems better not to search quite so assid-
uously for specific clues when a not unfamiliar general explication may account for most of the facts. Of course,
such an explication selectively shunts such "clues" onto the
sidetrack of insignificance, assuring in the end a degree of
ambiguity typical of Kafka's fiction, whether short or long. It
emerges most clearly and convincingly when one attempts
to explain what is inexplicable.

That pursuit: the attempt—maybe the addiction—to
explain the inexplicable is a topic that in quite specific terms
engages Kafka himself. He emphasizes the fatuity of it in a
cluster of parables from 1919 to 1923, thus a range that
includes as well "A Little Fable" and "Give It Up!" Extremely
prominent in this cluster is "Prometheus" (1919), a half-page
parable that draws on the mythological Titan who angered
Zeus by betraying the secret of fire to the human race; for
this transgression, or perhaps the hubris that fostered it, he
was horribly punished.

Kafka declares that there are four legends about Prometheus. According to the first, Prometheus was bound to a rock in the Caucasus, for betraying the divine secret of fire to humans; there the gods dispatched eagles to feed on his liver, which was continually renewed. According to the second, Prometheus's pain was such that he pressed himself deeper into the rock until he melded with it. In the third legend, Prometheus's treachery was forgotten over the millennia, by the gods, by the eagles, and himself. And in the fourth, everyone concerned grew weary of the meaningless affair. But the mass of rock remained, the inexplicability of which the legend sought to explain. Because the legend developed from a substratum of truth, Kafka explains — he is actually explicating his parable in the biblical fashion — the legend could only end in the inexplicable. Note that Kafka grants only a substratum of truth, not, as in most biblical parables, a pervasive, almost superobvious truth. What is almost superobvious about Kafka himself is his disdain for the possibility of unambiguous explication. His own rare explication is thus in itself highly ironic, a paradox.

Somewhat the same explication, namely that a certain amount of truth — of weary truth? — results in inexplicability, would appear suitable for "The Top" (1920), but here Kafka reverts to his usual omission of explication, even paradoxical explication. "The Top" presents a philosopher who hangs around where children are spinning tops. He is eager to chase down and seize a top while it is still spinning. For he thinks that comprehending such a small thing as the spinning of a top will enable him to comprehend everything. But on grasping a spinning top he holds in his hand only an inert piece of wood. That is his reward — the reward of his hope, it may be suggested — for attempting to explicate the inexplicable. Of course to make this explication work, it is necessary to equate the understanding of all things with the inexplicable — and one is thereupon into paradox again. Perhaps predictably, Marxist criticism of the parable establishes a polarity between static (the piece of wood) and dynamic (the spinning top), which represents the revolving earth. With this it is clear that Western interpretation is not alone in violating Kafka's own bias against attempting unambiguous explication of the inexplicable.

Fittingly enough, Kafka's final parable (1922–23) bears the title "On Parables"—fittingly both as a capstone and as an accurate title. In addition to parabolic discourse in which, like a Chinese box puzzle, parable is enclosed in parable, Kafka as the reflective narrator asserts that parables really only want to say that the incomprehensible is incomprehensible—and this "we" already know. Certainly we do if we have considered his representative parables, and especially those from the last two or three years of his life.

Conclusions

The fundamental quality that makes Kafka different — in his time almost uniquely different — from the received tradition of the nineteenth and early twentieth centuries is his abrogation, or more graphically, his collapsing of the aesthetic distance that was presumed to separate the writer from his reader. He does not merely vary it, now letting the reader come close to the work, now contriving to widen the distance again — he abolishes it entirely, from beginning to end. The reader is given Gregor Samsa turned into an insect as, even before, the story begins. Gregor does not become for a while less an insect, for a while more an insect, nor is his insectness revealed at the end — or anywhere else — to have been a dream or an illusion. Gregor dies an insect, with the dessicated body of an insect. Except in narrative retrospect, the reader has never seen him as anything else.

The continuing reaction of the reader to this seemingly unmediated closeness is to be shocked out of his or her capacity to reflect. One is obliged to confront the fictional catastrophe without the solace of contemplation that was earlier provided for by aesthetic distancing. Reflection, moreover, and analysis and interpretation are no longer external to the fiction. Those processes were formerly performed by the reader more or less at his leisure, but, with Kafka, they are part and parcel of the fiction itself. The reader's problem with authorial analysis and interpretation as performed by Kafka is that the processes and the results never seem fixed and definitive. They are repeated, modi-

151

fied, subjected to dialectics, to irony, to humor. So that the careful reader, probably to his discomfort, has learned to be wary of subscribing very wholeheartedly to such internal glosses, anticipating always a revision which, like its predecessors, may in any case affront his sense of logic — or simply prove all but impenetrable.[1]

Most often the differing authorial exegeses, each in turn purporting to clarify — the explications in "Before the Law" may be the most concentrated example — in sum reinforce the sense of ambiguity that the reader has already discovered for himself.[2] Many readers, not comfortable with ambiguity, will find themselves grasping almost haphazardly for narrative straws that can conceivably resolve ambiguity. The trouble is, most such grasps are not well conceived and most such straws are irrelevant, false. One is better advised to develop a tolerance, if not exactly an appreciation for Kafka's insistence on ambiguity. After all, the prolix, often-contradictory internal explication would itself militate against the likelihood of one's finding a "key" that would make it all simple and logical.

It is often said that Kafka offers two modes of description concurrently, that his realistic narration is masterfully interwoven with the fantastic, that this concurrence or simultaneity is indeed part of his effect, of his shock. This may have some truth in it, but the reader is advised not to assume that Kafka's presumed realism is necessarily to be equated with his report writing as an insurance investigator. He made no bones about his distaste for the naturalistic novel, that is, fictional realism. And often enough his presumed realism contains a sign of deformation, like the small defect in the castle representative's voice over the telephone. Or, while the snow may be realistic snow, the reader may well ponder the apparent absence of summer in the region of the castle and the village. And in fact there *was* something a little wrong with the snow: so little fell on the castle that was higher, so much on the village that was lower. The accumulated effect of these little, dubiously realistic discrepancies on the reader, whether duly noted or just sub- liminally recorded, is likely to be one of alienation, or maybe more accurately, a slightly desperate perplexity. Is every- thing that is read, one wonders — the descriptive-narrative as well as the analytical — to be subjected to doubt?

In his constant struggle for orientation, urged along by his perhaps wider familiarity with literature in which the fictional events or things "stand for" something else, the reader is apt to start finding supposed reference points in Kafka's writings. In a word, allegorizing — as do those who see the Emperor of China as standing for the Emperor of the Hapsburg realm, or the castle as standing for God, or the awful wound in the thigh of the country doctor's patient as standing for Christ's wounds. But people and things in Kafka's writing almost never stand for somebody or some- thing else, nor does the detail represent the generality. Rath- er Kafka aims directly at an overarching absolute meaning, and it is apt to be less than cosmic, more often focused squarely on the individual human being.

For that reason it is especially difficult to enlist Kafka postmortem in political-social movements that either inher- ently or doctrinally orient themselves to the mass rather than the individual. Not that he is naive about the suprain- dividual mass and how it tends to act and react. One thinks of the mouse people or perhaps, more chillingly, the min- ions, uniformed and not, of the castle. The point necessary to make here is that although Kafka was not ignorant or naive about social mass, mass is not a very prominent focus of his fiction. Not perhaps dynamism either, seen as the opposite of quiescence. It could be argued with some per- suasiveness that both Josef K. in *The Trial* and K. in *The Castle* would have been better off had they been less active.

Kafka's preference for orientation to the individual may

bring the reader to examine with especial stringency the apparent implication in, for example, "In the Penal Colony," that the *era* of the old commandant was superior to that of the new commandant. As far as that goes, were the good old days really better? Only in the most ironic sense, if one applies the autobiographical criterion, which is often more appropriate than the social or the Nietzschean. Similarly in "The New Advocate" one ought to examine closely the critical consensus that Dr. Bucephalus is a somewhat unwisely indulged survivor of a more vigorous, regrettably past, era. Or, in "A Country Doctor," that olden times were somehow better, when the church exerted a greater influence and a medical doctor was not called upon to do a priest's work. One's reference points are, in fact, individuals. The implications or the inferences transcend the individual. Those above probably are cautious enough if one keeps Kafka's preferred focus in mind. It would on the other hand seriously misrepresent Kafka to allegorize Josef K. or K. into an Everyman. They are not; they are fictional personae of Kafka himself — as indeed are most of his heroes.

Heroes, not heroines. The probably more accurate term, protagonist, still cannot obscure the fact that Josephine the Singer, a mouse after all, is the only female in a leading role. (A consideration of *all* the short stories and parables would yield one or two more female protagonists.) It is probably correct to say that for all of Kafka's revolutionary abolition of aesthetic distance in his prose fiction, in the question of fictional attitude toward women he is still very much an heir of the nineteenth century. A sympathetic, mutually admiring, frank, and wit-enlivened relationship, such as he enjoyed with his sister Ottla, seems to be precluded from his fiction. There are fleeting exceptions — perhaps the girl on the streetcar, even, more ambiguously, Amalia in *The Castle* — but most of Kafka's fictional women appear not only in subordinate roles but in the primary role of sex object. The fate of Amalia and her family for her refusal to *be* as well as *seem* a sex object to Sortini is instructive. Differently ambiguous in her role as both woman and sex object is the chief cook at the Hotel Occidental in *Amerika*: in the end she sacrifices her principles and Karl Rossmann as well while the head waiter fondles her hand. Therese Berchtold, the ingenue secretary-typist, is at the least a rather provocative flirt. And so on. Many of the women in Kafka's fiction — Leni comes to mind too — do not rise very far above the level of cliché.

Not necessarily sterile cliché. After all, the chief cook and Therese do play dual roles. Frieda in *The Castle*, for all her sexual athleticism, is in her fashion seeking a niche in the castle-dominated society — regaining her job as barmaid at the Herrenhof — quite as insistently as K. seeks to occupy the post of land surveyor. If the obstacles put in Frieda's way, because she is a woman, are different and possibly even more daunting, her pursuit of "justice" is as rational, as goal-directed, as resilient as that of K. — and more fruitful.

K.'s quest, flawed and misdirected as it sometimes is, is rational in comparison with the guilt-laden struggling of Josef K. and Karl Rossmann. The latter two questers, on a mundane level, are guilty of consistently bad judgment, not to mention, especially in the case of Josef K., snobbery. But above and beyond the mundane, their guilt is existential. Judgmental and moral lapses have nothing to do with it, except perhaps to deepen the irony that attends it. And is not existential guilt already by its very nature ironic? Nevertheless — though it is often vitiated by translation — Kafka here and generally makes generous additional use of irony. Unlike that of Thomas Mann, which is primarily inherent in the very narration itself, Kafka's irony is for the most part — aside from its relationship to existential guilt — specific and locatable. One has only to be receptive and sensitive to it.

The same may be said of his humor. To a degree it too is

an inevitable victim of translation, but it is even more a
victim of the repute in which Kafka is held as a writer of
striking earnestness. But this earnestness is well salted with
humor. Karl Rossmann's plight in the Brunelda menage is
lamentable, but it is funny as well. Josef K. is in an increasingly perilous relationship with the Court when with his
uncle he visits lawyer Huld, and yet his all too prompt seduction by Leni is not without its humorous side (and even if
Leni herself is little more than a one-dimensional cliché).

What remains to be said about Kafka's language as language may relate to the evident earnestness with which it
seems to emerge above all in English. But it relates also to its
remarkable balance, to its amplitude, and its irony. For by an
accident of linguistic history, Prague German writers wrote
the same German that they spoke and lived. That is, there
was no difference in level between the language they spoke
and the standard literary German in which they wrote. A
slightly archaizing tone, rich in ironic suggestion, permeates
Kafka's German; the effect, somewhat diluted, is discernible
as well in the English versions.

Notes

INTRODUCTION

1. Emanuel Frynta, *Kafka and Prague*, tr. Jean Layton (London: Batch-worth Press, 1960), p. 54.
2. He read a Kierkegaard anthology entitled *Buch des Richters* (Book of the Judge); entry of August 21, 1913. *The Diaries of Franz Kafka 1910–1913*, ed. Max Brod, tr. Joseph Kresh (New York: Schocken, 1948), p. 298. However, in a letter to Oskar Baum of October/Novem-ber 1917 he volunteers that he knows only "Fear and Trembling." *Briefe 1902–24* (New York: Schocken, 1958), p. 190.

1. EARLY PROSE: *DESCRIPTION OF A STRUGGLE*, "WEDDING PREPARATIONS IN THE COUNTRY," "THE JUDGMENT"

1. *Dearest Father: Stories and Other Writings*, tr. Ernst Kaiser and Eithne Wilkins (New York: Schocken, 1954), p. 6.
2. *Selected Short Stories*, tr. Willa and Edwin Muir (New York: Modern Library, 1952), p. 18.
3. Ibid.

2. *THE METAMORPHOSIS*, "THE STOKER"

1. Gustav Janouch, *Conversations with Kafka*, tr. Goronwy Rees (New York: New Directions, 1969), p. 55.
2. Cf. also Czech *sam*, "alone."
3. *Selected Short Stories*, p. 19.
4. Kafka to Kurt Wolff, October 25, 1915. *Briefe 1902–1924*, pp. 135–36.
5. *Proměna* (Stará Říše, Czechoslovakia: Dobré Dílo, 1929).
6. *Selected Short Stories*, p. 76.
7. Ibid., pp. 78, 79.

3. AMERIKA

1. Entry of October 8, 1917. *The Diaries of Franz Kafka 1914–1923*, tr. Martin Greenberg, with the cooperation of Hannah Arendt (New York: Schocken, 1949), p. 188.
2. But it has to be noted that, at least in contrast to K. in *The Trial*, Kafka denotes Karl Rossmann as "innocent." Diary entry of September 30, 1915; p. 132.
3. *Amerika*, tr. Edwin Muir (Norfolk, Conn.: New Directions, [1946]), p. 3. Muir immediately deletes Kafka's ironic thrust by transposing the adjective "poor" from Karl's parents, where the author had placed it, to Karl. The ironic point thus obscured is that Karl's parents were not poor at all but quite prosperous, as the author gradually reveals. It is difficult to assess just how much such tampering has contributed to the English-language reader's false impression that Kafka is relentlessly earnest.
4. The "Urereignis." Wolfgang Jahn, *Kafkas Roman "Der Verschollene" ("Amerika")*, (Stuttgart: Metzler, 1965), p. 14.
5. Peter Sedlacek, "August Strindberg und Franz Kafka. Versuch einer vergleichenden Betrachtung von Persönlichkeit und Werk" (Diss. Vienna, 1960), p. 131. Cited by Peter U. Beicken, *Franz Kafka. Eine kritische Einführung in die Forschung* (Frankfurt am Main: Athenaion, 1974), p. 256. But cf. Hartmut Binder, *Kafka-Kommentar* (Munich: Winkler, 1976), p. 78.
6. *Amerika*, p. 68.
7. Ibid., p. 71.
8. For example, by Jahn, pp. 19, 28. See also the more widely available Heinz Politzer, *Franz Kafka: Parable and Paradox* (Ithaca and London: Cornell University Press, 1966), p. 143. Politzer, while perceiving "the all too obvious symbolism," fails to pursue the motif implication. The apple is not there as just a static symbol.
9. *Amerika*, p. 252.
10. *Diaries 1914–23*, p. 132.
11. *Amerika*, p. 298.

4. THE TRIAL

1. *The Trial*, tr. Willa and Edwin Muir, revised; additional materials tr. E. M. Butler (New York: Modern Library, 1961), p. 3. Subsequent references are parenthesized in my text.
2. This runs counter to Max Brod's opinion that the fragment "District

Attorney" would have been placed much later, following chapter 7. For a proposed reordering of the chapters of *The Trial* (as well as of *Amerika*), see Herman Uyttersprot, *Eine neue Ordnung der Werke Kafkas? Zur Struktur von "Der Prozess" und "Amerika"* (Antwerp: C. de Vries-Brouwers, 1957).

3. The reference to personal responsibility has no warrant in the German original.

5. "IN THE PENAL COLONY," "A COUNTRY DOCTOR," "AN OLD MANUSCRIPT," "BUILDING THE GREAT WALL OF CHINA," "A REPORT FOR AN ACADEMY"

1. "A Country Doctor," in *The Penal Colony: Stories and Short Pieces*, tr. Willa and Edwin Muir (New York: Schocken, 1948), p. 136.

2. "An Old Manuscript," in *The Penal Colony: Stories and Short Pieces*, p. 147.

3. "A Report to an Academy" ("A Report for an Academy"), in *The Penal Colony: Stories and Short Pieces*, p. 183. Subsequent references are parenthesized in my text.

6. THE CASTLE

1. *The Castle*, tr. Willa and Edwin Muir, with additional materials tr. Eithne Wilkins and Ernst Kaiser (New York: Knopf, 1974), p. 14. Subsequent references are parenthesized in my text.

7. "INVESTIGATIONS OF A DOG," "THE BURROW," "A HUNGER ARTIST," "JOSEPHINE THE SINGER"

1. "Investigations of a Dog," in *The Great Wall of China: Stories and Reflections*, tr. Willa and Edwin Muir (New York: Schocken, 1946), p. 26. Subsequent references are parenthesized in my text.

2. "The Burrow," in *The Great Wall of China: Stories and Reflections*, pp. 80, 103.

3. For an extended development of the hypothetical personalized narrator, of which my remarks are an abbreviation, see Roy Pascal, *Kafka's Narrators: A Study of His Stories and Sketches* (Cambridge: Cambridge University Press, 1982).

CONCLUSIONS

1. Some of my concluding formulations are derived from Theodor W. Adorno, "Form und Gehalt des zeitgenössischen Romans," *Akzente*, 1, no. 5 (1954), 410–16, and Wilhelm Emrich, "Zur Ästhetik der modernen Dichtungen," *Akzente*, 1, no. 4 (1954), 371–87.
2. Not only the reader of course: a recent study proposes that the protagonist's inability to interpret his situation other than ambiguously is responsible for his destruction. Charles Bernheimer, *Flaubert and Kafka: Studies in Psychopoetic Structure*. (New Haven and London: Yale University Press, 1982), p. 189.

Bibliography

SELECT BIBLIOGRAPHY OF BOOKS IN ENGLISH

I. Works by Kafka

There are numerous reeditions, reprintings, and regatherings in both the United States and the United Kingdom. The following is meant to be helpful rather than exhaustive.

Amerika. Tr. Edwin Muir. Norfolk, Conn.: New Directions, [1946]; New York, 1962.

The Bridge. Tr. Willa and Edwin Muir. New York: Schocken, 1983.

The Castle. Tr. Willa and Edwin Muir. New York: Knopf, 1951; London: Secker & Warburg, 1953. With additional materials by Eithne Wilkins and Ernst Kaiser. New York: Knopf, 1954, 1974.

The Complete Stories. Ed. Nahum N. Glatzer. New York: Schocken, 1971, 1983.

The Country Doctor: A Collection of Fourteen Short Stories. Tr. Vera Leslie. Oxford: Counterpoint Publications, 1945.

Dearest Father: Stories and Other Writings. Tr. Ernst Kaiser and Eithne Wilkins. New York: Schocken, 1954.

Description of a Struggle. Tr. Tania and James Stern. New York: Schocken, 1958.

The Diaries of Franz Kafka 1910–13. Ed. Max Brod. Tr. Joseph Kresh. New York: Schocken, 1948.

The Diaries of Franz Kafka 1914–23. Tr. Martin Greenberg, with the cooperation of Hannah Arendt. New York: Schocken, 1949.

Franz Kafka [contains *The Trial, Amerika, The Castle, Metamorphosis*, "In the Penal Settlement," "The Great Wall of China," "Investigations of a Dog," "Letter to His Father," *The Diaries 1910–23*]. London: Secker & Warburg/Octopus, 1976.

A Franz Kafka Miscellany: Pre-Fascist Exile. Tr. Sophie Prombaum and G. Humphreys-Roberts. Rev. enl. 2nd. ed. New York: Twice a Year Press, 1946.

The Great Wall of China: Stories and Reflections. Tr. Willa and Edwin Muir. New York: Schocken, 1946, 1970.

I Am a Memory Come Alive: Autobiographical Writings of Franz Kafka. Ed. Nahum N. Glatzer. New York: Schocken, 1974.

Letter to His Father. Brief an den Vater. Bilingual ed. Tr. Ernst Kaiser and Eithne Wilkins. New York: Schocken, 1966.

Letters to Felice. Eds. Erich Heller and Jürgen Born. Tr. James Stern and Elisabeth Duckworth. New York: Schocken, 1973.

Letters to Friends, Family, and Editors. Ed. Max Brod. Tr. Richard and Clara Winston. New York: Schocken, 1977.

Letters to Milena. Ed. Willi Haas. Tr. Tania and James Stern. New York: Schocken, 1953; London: Secker & Warburg, 1953; Harmondsworth and New York: Penguin, 1983.

Letters to Ottla and the Family. Ed. Nahum N. Glatzer. Tr. Richard and Clara Winston. New York: Schocken, 1982.

Metamorphosis. Tr. A. L. Lloyd. New York: Vanguard, 1946. *The Metamorphosis.* Tr. and ed. Stanley Corngold. New York: Bantam, 1972.

Parables in German and English. Bilingual ed. New York: Schocken, 1947. *Parables and Paradoxes.* Bilingual ed. New York: Schocken, 1958, 1961, 1975.

The Penal Colony: Stories and Short Pieces. Tr. Willa and Edwin Muir. New York: Schocken, 1948, 1976.

The Penguin Complete Novels of Franz Kafka. Tr. Willa and Edwin Muir. Harmondsworth and New York: Penguin, 1983.

The Penguin Complete Short Stories of Franz Kafka. Ed. Nahum N. Glatzer. London: Allen Lane, 1983.

Selected Short Stories. Tr. Willa and Edwin Muir. New York: Modern Library, 1952.

Shorter Works [of] Franz Kafka. Tr. and ed. Malcolm Pasley. London: Secker & Warburg, 1973.

Stories 1904–24. Tr. J. A. Underwood. London and Sydney: Macdonald, 1981.

The Trial. Tr. Willa and Edwin Muir, with additional materials tr. E. M. Butler. New York: Knopf, 1957, 1978; New York: Modern Library, 1957, 1961, 1964. Tr. Douglas Scott and Chris Weller. London: Pan, 1977.

II. Works about Kafka

Anders, Günther. *Franz Kafka.* Tr. A. Steer and A. K. Thorlby. London: Bowes & Bowes, 1960.

Bauer, Johann. *Kafka and Prague*. Tr. P. S. Falla. New York: Praeger, 1971.

Beck, Evelyn Torton. *Kafka and the Yiddish Theater: Its Impact on His Work*. Madison, Milwaukee, and London: University of Wisconsin Press, 1971.

Bernheimer, Charles. *Flaubert and Kafka. Studies in Psychopoetic Structure*. New Haven and London: Yale University Press, 1982.

Bridgwater, Patrick. *Kafka and Nietzsche*. Bonn: Bouvier, 1974.

Brod, Max. *Kafka: A Biography*. Tr. G. Humphreys-Roberts. New York: Schocken, 1947. 2nd. enl. ed., tr. G. Humphreys-Roberts and Richard Winston, 1960, 1963.

Canetti, Elias. *Kafka's Other Trial: The Letters to Felice*. Tr. Christopher Middleton. New York: Schocken, 1974.

Carrouges, Michel. *Kafka versus Kafka*. Tr. Emmett Parker. University, Ala.: University of Alabama Press, 1968.

Collins, R. G., and Kenneth McRobbie, eds. *New Views on Franz Kafka*. Winnipeg: University of Manitoba Press, 1970.

Corngold, Stanley. *The Commentator's Despair: The Interpretation of Kafka's "Metamorphosis."* Fort Washington, N.Y. and London: Kennikat Press, 1973.

Deleuze, Gilles, and Félix Guattari. *Kafka: Toward a Minor Literature*. Tr. Dana Polan. Minneapolis: University of Minnesota Press, 1986.

Eisner, Pavel. *Franz Kafka and Prague*. Tr. Lowry Nelson and René Wellek. New York: Arts, 1950.

Emrich, Wilhelm. *Franz Kafka: A Critical Study of His Writings*. Tr. Sheema Z. Buehne. New York: Ungar, 1968.

Fickert, Kurt J. *Kafka's Doubles*. Bern, Frankfurt am Main, and Las Vegas: Peter Lang, 1979.

Flores, Angel. *A Kafka Bibliography 1908–76*. New York: Gordian Press, 1976.

_____, ed. *Explain to Me Some Stories of Kafka. Complete Texts with Explanations*. New York: Gordian Press, 1983.

_____, ed. *The Kafka Debate: New Perspectives for Our Time*. Staten Island, N.Y.: Gordian Press, 1977.

_____, ed. *The Kafka Problem*. New York: Octagon Books, 1963; reprint, New York: Gordian Press, 1975.

_____, ed. *The Problem of "The Judgment,"* with a new tr. of "The Judgment" by Malcolm Pasley. New York: Gordian Press, 1977.

_____, and Homer Swander, eds. *Franz Kafka Today*. Madison: University of Wisconsin Press, 1964.

Foulkes, A. P. *The Reluctant Pessimist: A Study of Franz Kafka*. The Hague and Paris: Mouton, 1967.

Frynta, Emanuel. *Kafka and Prague*. Tr. Jean Layton. London: Batchworth Press, 1960.

Glatzer, Nahum N. *The Loves of Franz Kafka*. New York: Schocken, 1986.

Goodman, Paul. *Kafka's Prayer*. New York: Stonehill, 1947.

Gray, Ronald. *Franz Kafka*. Cambridge: Cambridge University Press, 1973.

_____. *Kafka's Castle*. Cambridge: Cambridge University Press, 1956.

Greenberg, Martin. *The Terror of Art: Kafka and Modern Literature*. New York and London: Basic Books, 1968.

Gruša, Jiří. *Franz Kafka of Prague*. Tr. Eric Mosbacher. London: Secker & Warburg, 1983.

Hall, Calvin S., and Richard E. Lind. *Dreams, Life, and Literature: A Study of Franz Kafka*. Chapel Hill: University of North Carolina Press, 1970.

Hamalian, Leo, comp. *Franz Kafka: A Collection of Criticism*. New York: McGraw-Hill, 1974.

Hayman, Ronald. *Kafka: A Biography*. New York: Oxford University Press, 1982.

Heller, Erich. *The Basic Kafka*. New York: Pocket Books, 1979.

_____. *Franz Kafka*. New York: Viking, 1975.

Heller, Peter. *Dialectics and Nihilism: Essays on Lessing, Nietzsche, Mann, and Kafka*. Amherst: University of Massachusetts Press, 1966.

Hibberd, John. *Kafka in Context*. London: Studio Vista, 1975.

Hughes, Kenneth, ed. and tr. *Franz Kafka: An Anthology of Marxist Criticism*. Hanover and London: University Press of New Zealand, 1981.

Jaffe, Adrian. *The Process of Kafka's "Trial."* Lansing: Michigan State University Press, 1967.

Janouch, Gustav. *Conversations with Kafka*. Tr. Goronwy Rees. New York: New Directions, 1969, 1971.

Kirchberger, Lida. *Franz Kafka's Use of Law in Fiction*. New York, Bern, and Frankfurt am Main: Peter Lang, 1986.

Kuna, Franz. *Franz Kafka: Literature as Corrective Punishment*. Bloomington and London: Indiana University Press, 1974; London: Paul Elek, 1974.

_____, ed. *On Kafka: Semi-Centenary Perspectives*. New York: Barnes & Noble, 1976.

Levi, Mijal. *Kafka and Anarchism*. New York: Revisionist Press, 1972.

Marill, René [R. M. Albérès], and Pierre de Boisdeffre. *Kafka: The Torment of Man*. Tr. Wade Baskin. New York: Philosophical Library, 1968.

Marson, Eric. *Kafka's "Trial": The Case Against Josef K.*. St. Lucia: University of Queensland Press, 1975.

Neider, Charles. *The Frozen Sea: A Study of Franz Kafka*. New York: Oxford University Press, 1948.

Norris, Margot. *Beasts of the Modern Imagination: Darwin, Nietzsche, Kafka, Ernst, and Lawrence*. Baltimore: Johns Hopkins University Press, 1985.

Osborne, Charles. *Kafka*. New York: Barnes & Noble, 1967.

Pascal, Roy. *Kafka's Narrators: A Study of His Stories and Sketches*. Cambridge: Cambridge University Press, 1982.

Pasley, Malcolm. *Catalogue of the Kafka Centenary Exhibition 1983*. Oxford: Bodleian Library, 1983.

Pawel, Ernest. *The Nightmare of Reason: A Life of Franz Kafka*. New York: Farrar, Straus and Giroux, 1984.

Politzer, Heinz. *Franz Kafka: Parable and Paradox*. Ithaca and London: Cornell University Press, 1966.

Rhein, Phillip H. *The Urge to Live: A Comparative Study of Franz Kafka's "Der Prozess" and Albert Camus' "L'Etranger."* Chapel Hill: University of North Carolina Press, 1964, 1966.

Robert, Marthe. *Franz Kafka's Loneliness*. Tr. Ralph Manheim. London: Faber & Faber, 1982. Also translated as *As Lonely as Franz Kafka*. New York and London: Harcourt Brace Jovanovich, 1982.

Robertson, Ritchie. *Kafka: Judaism, Politics, and Literature*. Oxford: Clarendon Press, 1985.

Rolleston, James. *Kafka's Narrative Theater*. University Park and London: Pennsylvania State University Press, 1974.

———, ed. *Twentieth Century Interpretations of "The Trial."* Englewood Cliffs: Prentice-Hall, 1976.

Roy, Gregor. *Kafka's "The Trial," "The Castle," and Other Works: A Critical Commentary*. New York: Monarch Press, 1966.

Sharp, Daryl. *The Secret Raven: Conflict and Transformation in the Life of Franz Kafka*. Toronto: Inner City Books, 1980.

Sheppard, Richard. *On Kafka's "Castle": A Study*. New York: Barnes & Noble, 1973.

Sokel, Walter H. *Franz Kafka*. New York: Columbia University Press, 1966.

Spann, Meno. *Franz Kafka*. Boston: Twayne, 1976.

Spilka, Mark. *Dickens and Kafka: A Mutual Interpretation*. Bloomington: Indiana University Press, 1963.

Stern, J. P., ed. *The World of Franz Kafka*. New York: Holt, Rinehart and Winston, 1980.

Sussman, Henry. *Franz Kafka: Geometrician of Metaphor*. Madison, Wis.: Coda Press, 1979.

Tauber, Herbert. *Franz Kafka: An Interpretation of His Works*. New Haven: Yale University Press, 1948.

Thorlby, Anthony. *Kafka: A Study*. London: Heinemann, 1972.

Tiefenbrun, Ruth. *Moment of Torment: An Interpretation of Franz Kafka's Short Stories*. Carbondale and Edwardsville: Southern Illinois University Press, 1973.

Urzidil, Johannes. *There Goes Kafka*. Tr. Harold A. Basilius. Detroit: Wayne State University Press, 1968.

Wagenbach, Klaus. *Franz Kafka: Pictures of a Life*. Tr. Arthur S. Wensinger. New York: Pantheon, 1984.

Index

"Advocates," 12
alienation as theme, 27, 29–31
ambiguity, 17, 98, 137–38, 154–55
  in *The Castle*, 105, 109, 123, 124, 154–55
  in the parables, 146, 148, 149–50, 152
  in *The Trial*, 58, 61, 80, 84, 85, 86
Amerika, 35–36, 39–53, 58, 155
  interpretations of, 39, 47–48, 50–51
  Kafka's opinion of, 36, 40
  seduction-expulsion-fall theme in, 41–48, 50, 52, 70, 114
  structure of, 40–41, 43, 51, 53
  writing and publication of, 7, 36, 38
animal stories, 101, 125–32, 135, 144–45
  autobiographical elements in, 125

Bauer, Felice, 8, 17, 21
  and Kafka, engagement of, 8, 9, 10, 19, 55, 59, 84, 93, 103
"Before the Law," 141–43, 147, 152
Bloch, Grete, 9
Brod, Max, 5, 8, 12, 13, 15, 35, 122, 138
  as editor and publisher of Kafka's works, 7, 18, 38, 39, 41, 48, 51, 55, 56, 72, 86, 125, 146

  and Kafka, encouragement of, 6–7, 16–17
"Building the Great Wall of China," 9, 99–100, 145
burlesque, 110, 116
"Burrow, The," 13, 130–32
  interpretations of, 131–32

caricature, 35
Castle, The, 40, 103–24
  autobiographical elements in, 103–4, 121, 154–55
  editions of, 117
  humor in, 110
  interpretations of, 104, 107, 122–24, 153
  themes of, 105–6, 116–20, 123
  writing of, 10, 12, 13, 103
character(s), 29–35, 38, 75, 113, 116, 154–55
  autobiographical, 15–16, 17, 19, 21–22, 27, 29–31, 46, 55, 64, 78, 84, 90, 102, 103, 104, 121, 125–26, 129–30, 131–32, 140–41, 143–44, 154
  Hermann Kafka as model for, 2, 10–11, 22, 29–31, 46, 145
  models for, 2, 11, 21–22, 28, 30–31, 104
Coester, Otto (illustrator), 30
"Conversation with the Suppli-cant," 16

"Country Doctor, A," 9, 93–98, 143, 154
  humor in, 96–97
  interpretations of, 97–98
  writing and publication of, 93
criticism. *See* Interpretations of Kafka's works
"Crossbreed, A," 144–45

Description of a Struggle, 7, 15–16, 19
  structure of, 15
  theme in, 15–16
diaries of Franz Kafka, 7, 8, 21, 27, 48
Dickens, Charles, 39–40, 51
distance, aesthetic, 29, 32, 87, 151, 154
dream quality in Kafka's works, 21, 25, 36, 39, 48, 56, 66, 85, 93–94, 97
  in *Amerika*, 39, 48
  in *The Castle*, 107–8
  in *The Metamorphosis*, 29, 56
  in *The Trial*, 56, 66, 85
Dymant, Dora, 13

Eisner, Minze, 12
exploitation as theme, 41–42, 50, 53, 109–12

fantasy, 16, 49–50, 111, 152
"Fear and Trembling" (Kierkegaard), 8
Franklin, Benjamin, 40
Freud, Sigmund, 11, 84, 123
  See also Interpretations of Kafka's works, Freudian

"Give It Up," 12, 147–48

guilt as theme, 27, 60–61, 64, 77, 88–89, 91–92, 119–20, 123, 155

humor, 29, 30, 31, 51, 96–98, 102, 126, 137, 152, 155–56
  in *The Castle*, 110
  in the parables, 143
  in *The Trial*, 55–56, 58, 59, 63, 68, 75, 82
  See also Burlesque, Irony, Parody, Satire
"Hunger Artist, A," 132–35, 136
  themes of, 134
  writing and publication of, 12, 13
"Hunter Gracchus, The," 9
Hyperion, 16

illustrations of Kafka's works, 30
"Imperial Message, An," 100, 145
  See also "Message from the Emperor, A"
inadequacy as theme, 27
interpretations of Kafka's works, 29–30, 35, 37, 39, 47–48, 50–53, 78–82, 92, 97–98, 104, 107, 122–23, 129, 131–32, 141–50, 151–52
  Christian, 92, 98, 122–23, 133
  Freudian, 11, 46, 97, 122, 123–24
  Marxist, 53, 62, 65, 84, 137–38, 142, 149–50
  See also under titles of individual works
"In the Penal Colony," 9, 87–93, 94, 143, 154
"Investigations of a Dog," 12, 125–30
  interpretations of, 129–30
  publication of, 12
irony, 17–18, 21, 31–32, 35, 39, 52, 101, 115, 117, 152, 155–56

in "A Hunger Artist," 132–35
in "Investigations of a Dog," 125–30
in the parables, 140, 142–44, 146, 149
in *The Trial*, 60, 83, 84, 85
isolation as theme, 27

"Jackals and Arabs," 9
Jahn, Wolfgang, 43
Jesenská, Milena, 12
   as translator of Kafka's works, 12, 103–4
"Josephine the Singer, or the Mouse Folk," 135–38
   writing and publication of, 13
Judaism, 2, 13
   Kafka's attitude toward, 7, 11
"Judgment, The," 8, 18–25, 39, 99
   names in, significance of, 19, 21
   relationships in, 21–22, 29, 31
   writing and publication of, 18, 27, 36

Kafka, Franz, 1–13
   childhood and education of, 2–5, 7
   engagements of, 8, 9, 10, 12, 15, 19, 55, 59, 84, 93, 103
   and his father, relationship between, 2–4, 6, 7, 9, 10–11, 13
   health of, 5, 9, 10, 12–13, 93, 125, 132
   insurance career of, 5–7, 9, 12–14
   and marriage, fear of, 8, 10, 84
   self-criticism of, 12, 15–16, 19, 27, 36, 40, 73, 93
   sisters of, 2, 10, 13
Kafka, Hermann (father), 1–4, 6, 7, 9, 10–11, 13

   as model for characters in Franz Kafka's works, 2, 10–11, 29–31, 145
Kafka, Julie Löwy (mother), 2–3
Kierkegaard, Sören, 8

law, Kafka's interest in, 5, 78
letters of Franz Kafka, 8, 10–12, 15
"Letter to His Father" 10–11
light and darkness, 35, 80–84
"Little Fable, A," 146–47, 148
"Little Woman, A," 13
Lost Without Trace (early title of *Amerika*), 38, 39
   writing and publication of, 7, 8, 38

Mann, Thomas, 122, 155
"Message from the Emperor, A," 9
   See also "Imperial Message, An"
Metamorphosis, The, 18, 27–35, 39, 58, 59, 151
   characterization in, 29–32
   interpretations of, 29–30, 35
   Kafka's opinion of, 27
   structure of, 28
   themes of, 27, 29–30
   writing and publication of, 8, 27, 36
metaphor, 21, 23, 77, 104, 138
music motif, 28, 33, 34, 44, 49, 127–28, 135–36

names, significance of, 1, 52, 59, 68, 96, 98, 104, 105, 126, 130
   in *The Castle*, 109–10, 121, 122
   in "The Judgment," 19, 21
   in *The Metamorphosis*, 27–28
   in "Wedding Preparations in the Country," 17, 27–28

narrative viewpoint. *See* Point of
    view
narrator as Kafka-persona, 15–16,
    17, 19, 27, 29–31, 46, 90, 102,
    104, 154
  in the animal stories, 125–31
  in "The Burrow," 130, 131–32
  in *The Castle*, 103
  in "Investigations of a Dog," 125–
    26, 129–30
  in "The Judgment," 21–22
  in the parables, 140–41, 143–44
  in *The Trial*, 55, 64, 78, 84
naturalism, 4, 36, 39, 53, 84, 152
"Neighbor, The," 10, 143–44
"New Advocate, The," 154
  See also "New Attorney, The"
"New Attorney, The," 143
  See also "New Advocate, The"
Nietzsche, Friedrich, 92–93, 143,
    154

"Old Manuscript, An," 98–99, 100
"On Parables," 12, 150
"On the Tram," 140–41

parables, 12, 45–46, 65, 97, 100,
    113, 139–50
  autobiographical elements in,
    141, 143, 145
  defined, 139–40
  interpretations of, 141–44, 146–
    50, 152
  in *The Trial*, 75, 77–80, 141
paradox, 67, 85, 102, 149
parody, 39, 50, 51, 92
picaresque novel, 52
point of view, 16, 17–18, 22, 27, 87,
    93, 95, 99, 100, 136–37
  in *Description of a Struggle*, 15

in the parables, 140–41, 143–44,
    145–47
Poláková, Milena Jesenská
  See Jesenská, Milena
Prague, 1, 6, 18
  as setting for stories, 16, 87
"Prometheus," 148–49

quest as theme, 17, 104, 123, 155

religion, 83–84, 85, 92, 122–23, 133
  See also Judaism
"Report for an Academy," 9, 101–2,
    125, 129

satire, 111, 118–19, 123
seduction as theme, 37–38, 42–48
settings, 16, 21, 40, 49, 87
spirituality versus materialism, 33,
    35
Starke, Ottomar (illustrator), 30
"Stoker, The," 29, 35–38
  and *Amerika*, 35, 39–41, 43
  interpretations of, 37
  translation of, 12
  writing and publication of, 8, 35–
    36
structure, 15–17, 22, 28
  in *Amerika*, 40–41, 43, 51, 53
  in *The Castle*, 112–13
  in *Description of a Struggle*, 15–
    16
  in *The Trial*, 56, 73, 86
style, 16, 156
surrealistic elements in Kafka's
    works, 25, 36
symbols, 33, 34, 38, 46, 81, 96, 104

themes, 15–17, 37–38, 50, 53, 77,
    84, 88–89, 91–92, 94, 99, 134
  in *Amerika*, 41–48, 50, 52, 70

in *The Castle*, 105, 116–20, 123
in *The Metamorphosis*, 27, 29–30
in *The Trial*, 58, 60–62, 65, 77, 86, 92
"Top, The," 12, 149–50
translation of Kafka's works, 12, 30, 34, 63, 96, 105, 117, 118, 128, 130, 132, 133, 146, 156
Trial, The, 9, 40, 55–86, 89, 95, 96, 104, 141
    autobiographical elements in, 55, 64, 84, 90
    humor in, 55–56, 58, 59, 63, 68, 75, 82
    interpretations of, 62, 65, 78–82, 84, 153
    Kafka's opinion of, 55, 73
    politics in, 56–57, 84–85
    structure of, 56, 73, 86

themes of, 58, 60–62, 65, 77, 86, 92, 114
writing and publication of, 9, 87

unfinished works, 7, 15, 16, 103
utopias, 48, 52

"Wedding Preparations in the Country," 16–18, 19, 30
    names in, 27–28
    structure of, 16
    unfinished versions of, 7, 16
Werner, Marie, 3
Wohryzek, Julie, 10, 12, 103
Wolff, Kurt, 36, 93
women characters, 154–55

Yiddish theater, 7, 134